Research Methodsfor Beginners

Academic Scholarly Research Guide

Dr R Naveen Kumar

Made with ♥ on the Notion Press Platformwww.notionpress.com

This book is dedicated to all the good hearts who supported in making this book aremarkable reading aid.

Contents

Foreword

The genesis of this book can be traced over many years as several of us at the Academic Collection strove to define the very rich topic of collecting research aid in a way that could be embraced by both specialists and a curious general public. As is always the case in bringing a publication of this kind to light, many individuals and organizations should be acknowledged and thanked. Research insights were invaluable in setting us on a path to successfully organizing the presentations and later the chapters of our book.

The fact that displays in this book – much of it being public in nature for understanding the research concepts – often impacted the daily life of audiences other than gatherers. All of these issues, and more, are addressed by the authors who contributed to this volume.

Name of the author of the Foreword Dr R Naveen KumarCredentials

Date 12/01/2023

Preface

"This book is a great source of information to the readers who wish to gainknowledge in the research platform"

Dr R Naveen Kumar served as a full-time teaching faculty at Indian and Foreign Universities. He obtained his BSc in Computer Science from Bharathiar University and MBA from Anna University. His research degree PhD awarded from Karpagam University in Management. He holds 14 Years of teaching experience in India and Foreign Countries. He authored 5 books, published research papers in reputed Journals, and presented research papers at International and National Conferences. His interests found in enterprise development, mobile commerce, and digital marketing. He is an active personality of various associations and reviewing members of different boardswidely. He believed that modern business thoughts would change the enterprising arena, and he uses them to inspire and empower young people fortheir references.

Dr. V. Ramadevi has 13 years of experience in teaching and research. Her interest in research and guidance to scholars made her produce 3 Ph.D. candidates. She has published a good number of papers in popular research forums. She obtained her research degree PhD from Karpagam University in the year 2013 with a great knowledge of research practicality. She is optimistic and goal-oriented to achieve the desired outcomes. Her contributionto the research in the life of scholars is countless in bringing the best out of them.

Dr. M. Meenakshi Saratha, M.Com., M.Phil., MBA., PGDCA., Ph.D., Associate Professor of Commerce CS & IT. She has 15 years of experience in teaching and research. She has been awarded a Doctoral degree by Madurai

Kamaraj University in the year 2008, She also has completed MBA in Finance during the year 2009 at Mother Teresa Women's University, Kodaikanal. She has been conferred with the Degree of Philosophy in Commerce at Saraswathi Narayanan College in the year 2002, secured the degree PGDCA in 2004 at Manonmaniam Sundaranar University and a Degree of Master of Commerce in The Madura College (Evening), Madurai during the year 2001.

Unit 1: The Nature of ResearchThe meaning and Characteristics of Research

According to Kaoul (1984:10), then term "research "is defined as,

"A systematic attempt to obtain answers to meaningful questions about phenomena or events through the application of scientific procedures. It is an objective impartial, empirical or logical analysis and recording of controlled observations that may lead to the development of generalizations, principles or theories".

Research may result to some extent in prediction and control of events that may be consequences or of specific phenomena. The above definition ascertains the fact that a research is **the search for knowledge through objective and systematic method of finding solution to a problem,** a scientific endeavor that seeks to integrate and systematize its findings and concerned with the objective verification of generalizations based on logical analyses of problems with the help appropriate methodologies.

Characteristics of Research

According to best (1977:9) research has the following basic characteristics.

- ***Research is directed toward the solution of a problem.*** It may attempt to answer a question or to determine the relation between two or more variables.
- ***Research emphasizes the development of generalization, principles, or theories*** what will be helpful in predicting future occurrences.
- ***Research is based upon observation experiences or empirical evidence.*** Research *rejects revelation and dogma as methods of establishing knowledge* and accepts only what can be verified by observation.

- ***Research demands accurate observation and description the researcher uses quantitative numerical measuring devices, the most precise means of description.***
- Although research activity may by at times be somewhat random and unsystematic it is ***more often characterized by carefully designed procedures, always applying rigorous analysis.*** Although trial and error are often involved, research is rarely a blind, shotgun investigation – trying something to see what happens.
- ***Research requires expertise***. The researcher knows what is already known about the problem and how others have investigated it. He has searched the related literature carefully. He is also thoroughly grounded in the terminology, the concepts and the technical skill necessary to understand and analyses the data that he gathers.
- ***Research strives to be objective and logical, applying every possible test to validate the procedures employed the data collected and the conclusions reached.*** The researcher attempts to eliminate personal bias.
- ***Research is characterized by parent and unhurried activity.*** It is rarely that the researcher accepts disappointment and discouragement as he pursues the answers to difficult questions.
- ***Research is carefully recorded and reported***. The written report and accompanying data are made available to the scrutiny of other scholars. Any competent scholar will have the information necessary to analyze, evaluate, and even replicate the study.

1.2 Objectives of Research

The main objective of research is ***to discover answers to questions through the application of scientific procedures.*** In particular, r*esearch is conducted to find out the truth which is hidden and which has not been discovered as yet.* Though each research study has its own specific purpose, we may think or research objectives as falling into either of the following broad groupings.

- To gain familiarity with a phenomenon or to achieve new insights into it (studies with this object in view are termed as ***exploratory or formulative research studies***,)
- To portray accurately the characteristics of a particular individual, situation or a group (studies with this object in view are known as***descriptive research studies***),
- To determine the frequency with which something occurs or with which it is associated with something else (studies with this object in view are known as ***diagnostic research studies***),
- To test a hypothesis of a causal relationship between variables such studies are known as ***hypothesis –testing research studies***).
- Research is intended to equip the researcher with the following scholarly

1.3. Motivation in Research

People are motivated to conduct researches for a number of reasons. According to kothari (1990:2), the possible motives for doing research may emanate from one or more of the following:

- Desire to get a research degree along with its consequential benefits.
- Desire to face the challenge solving the unsolved problems i.e. concernover practical problems initiates' research.
- Desire to get intellectual joy of doing some creative work.
- Desire to be of service to society.
- To meet government directives or policies or other employmentconditions.

1.4. Human Inquiry and science:

Inquiry is a natural activity. People seek general understanding about the world around them. Much of what people know, they know by agreement (Agreement Reality) rather than by direct, personal experience \experiential reality). In day – to –day inquiry, we often make mistakes, but scientific inquiry offers protection against such mistakes: Whereas we often observe inaccurately, such errors are avoided in science by making observation a careful and deliberate activity. Sometimes we jump to general conclusions on the basis of only a few observations, but scientists avoid such overgeneralization through Replication, **i'e repeating studies.** Once a conclusion has been reached, we sometimes ignore evidence that contradicts that conclusion, only paying attention to evidence that confirms our initial conclusion. Whenever we are confronted with contradictory evidence, all of us endeavor to explain away the contradictions. Often this involves assuming facts not actually observed i.e deduced information.

Scientists, on the other hand, commit themselves to a set of observations to be made regardless of whether a pattern seems to emerge early. They also make further observation to test those assumptions. Sometimes people simply reasonillogically. Scientist avoids this by being as careful and as deliberate in their reasoning as in their observation. Moreover, the, public nature of science means that scientist has their colleagues liking over their shoulders. This critical role of colleagues also protects scientists from being ego-involved in their conclusions. Where people often decide they understand something and stop looking from new answers, scientists as a group, ultimately regard all issues as open Finally, science has no place for the common human conclusion that some things are ultimately unexplainable or unknowable.

Scientific theory and research address what is not what should be. Theory should not be confused with philosophy or belief. As such for instance, social science focused on logical and consistent regularities in associated initials. While social scientist observes human aggregates, they are primarily interested in finding relationships that connect variables. Whether human social behavior can be studied scientifically has been debated for some time. It can! The traditional image of science includes theory, operationalization, and observation. This is not, however, an accurate picture of how scientific research is actually done. Science is a process involving an alternation of induction and deduction, and it through these logical methods that social scientific theory and research are linked. Induction is the development of generalizations or theories from specific observations, while. Deduction is the development of specific expectations or hypotheses from generalizations or theories.

1.5. Types of Research

Different authorities classify research differently. The classification of research is based on the objectives or a purpose the researches intend to accomplish is shown below.

Applied Vs Pure research. Research can be roughly classified as *applied (or action) or pure (or fundamentals or basic).* **Applied research** is research with findings that can be *applied to solve social problems of immediate concern.* Applied research *seeks to find a solution for an immediate problem facing a society or an industrial business organization.* Applied research covers a ***wide range of social science areas***, including education, racial integration drug addiction and abuse alcoholism, crime and delinquency, women in the labor force, and problems of the aged. On the other hand, and, **pure research** is mainly concerned *with generalizations and with the formulation of the theory.* Itinvolves *developing and testing theories and hypotheses that are intellectually interesting to the investigator and might thus have some social application inthe future,* but have no application to social problem in the present time researchconcerning some natural phenomenon or relating to pure mathematics are examples of pure or basic research. Similarly, research studies, concerning human behavior carried with a view to make generalizations about humanbehavior, are also examples of basic research.

Descriptive Vs analytical research. Some scholars classify research as descriptive and analytical. **Descriptive research** includes surveys and fact- finding, enquiries of different kinds. The major purpose of descriptive research is description of the state of affairs as it exists at present, in descriptive research;the researcher has no control over the variables. He or she can only report what has happened or what is happening. Most expost-facto research projects, designed in the fields of social science and business are based on descriptive research studies. For instance, if a researcher intends to measure the frequency of shopping, preference of people to discover causes or loge the similar data then he/she is applying descriptive research. Descriptive research utilizes survey methods of all kinds. On the other hand, in **analytical research**, the researcher uses foots or information already available, and analyzes these to make a criticalevolution of the material.

Quantitative Vs Qualitative research: Some authorities divide research in to quantitative and qualitative. **Quantitative research** is based on the measurement of quantity or amount. It is applicable to phenomena that can be, expressed terms of quantity. **Qualitative research** on the other hand, is ***concerned with qualitative phenomenon- phenomenon relating to or involving quality or kind.*** For example, studies relating to human behavior fall in to this category of research. Qualitative research aims at *discovering the underlying motives and desires* by applying the techniques that include focus group interviews, in depth interviews, word association tests, sentencecompletion tests, story completion tests and similar other projective techniques. ***Attitude or opinion research*** i.e, research designed to find out how people feel or what they about a particular subject or institution is also qualitative research.

Conceptual Vs empirical research. Research can also be divided into conceptual and empirical. While conceptual research relies on some abstract ideas or theory, empirical research relies on experience or observation. Conceptual research is generally used by philosophers and thinkers to develop new concepts or to reinterpret existing ones. On the other hand, empiricalresearch is generally used by investigators who are interested in coming up with conclusions which are capable of being verified by observation or experiment. Itis data- base research and sometimes called as" experimental" research.

Some other types of research. All other types of research are variations of one or more of the above types, based on either the purpose of research, or the time required to accomplish research, or the environment in which research is done, or on the basis of some other similar factor.

From the point of view of time, we can think of research either as *one-time research or longitudinal research.* In the former case, the research is confined to a single-time period, whereas in the latter case the research is carried on over several time periods.

Research can be *field- setting research or laboratory research or simulation research,* ***depending upon the environment*** in which it is to be carried out.

Research can be as wellbeing understood as ***clinical or diagnostic research***. Such research follows case-study methods or in depth approaches to reach the basic causal relations. Such studies usually go droop into the courses of thingsor events that interest us. Using very small samples and very deep probing data gathering devices.

Historical research is a type of descriptive research that attempts to establish facts through meaningful and organized record of events so as to derive conclusions concerning past events. The purpose of historical research is to find connections between events in the past and variables in the present by means of critical review of evidences.

Research can also be classified as ***conclusion- oriented and decision*** – oriented in conclusion-oriented research, the researcher has a freedom to pick up a problem and to redesign the esquire as he/she proceeds and to conceptualize it as he/she wishes. In decision –oriented research, however, the researcher is not free to embark upon research according to his/her inclination as it is geared towards decision –making process. Operations research is an example of decision-oriented research since it is a scientific method of providing executive departments with a quantitative basis for decisions regarding operations under their control.

Tracer study (follow-up study): It is a type of explanatory study that aims at investigating the subsequent development of individual of individual or unit after a specified treatment or condition. Tracer study is used to establish patterns of change in the past so as to predict future patterns or conditions by analyzing data collected about subjects and environment. For example, researcher can conduct a tracer study concerning the outputs (former graduates) of Addis Ababa commercial college. This will help him/her to investigate or understand whether all of its graduates are employed or not, whether there is a mismatch between the raining he graduates received and the type of jobs they are handing and whether there is a need for changes in the college's curricula, programs, training methods, and training faculties to mention some of them only.

1.6 Differences in Underlying Research Techniques, ResearchMethods, and Research Methodology

1.6. 1. Research Methods Vs Research Techniques

Authorities have tried differentiating between research methods and research techniques. In this regard, kothari (1990:9) has succinctly put their difference asfollows. ***Research techniques*** refer to the *behavior and instruments we use in performing research operations* such as making observations, recording data, techniques of processing data and the like. ***Research methods*** refer to the*behavior and instruments used in selecting and constructing research technique*. For instance, the difference between methods and techniques of data collection can better be understood from the details given in the following chart.

Type	Methods	Techniques
1.Library research	(i) analysis of historical records	Recording of notes, content analysis, tape and film listening and analysis
	(ii) Analysis of	Statically compilations

	documents	and manipulations, reference and abstract guides, content analysis.
2. Field Research	(1) Non participant direct observation	Observation behavioral scales cards, etc.
	(ii) participant observation (iii) Mass observation	Interaction recording, possible use of tape recorders, photographic techniques. Recording mass behavior, interview using independent observers in public places.
	(iv) Mail questionnaire	Identification of social and economic back ground or responder scales.
	(V) Opinionnaire	Use of attitude scales, projective techniques, use of respondents.
	(vi) Personal interview	Interview uses a detailed schedule with open and closed questions
	(vii) Focused interview	Interviews focus attention upon a given experience and its effects.
	(Viii) Group interview	Small group of respondents are interviewed simultaneously.
	(ix) Telephone	Used as a survey technique for information and for discerning opinion; may also be used a follow up of questionnaire.
	X case study and life history	Cross sectional collection of data for intensive analysis character.

3. Laboratory research	Small group study of random behavior plays and role analysis.	Use of audio –visual recording device use of observers, etc.

From what has been stated above, we can say that methods are more general. It is methods that Generate techniques. However, in practice, the two terms are taken as interchangeable and when we talk research methods we to, by implication, include research techniques within their compass.

1.6.2. Research Methods Vs Research Methodology

There is a clear-cut demarcation between research methods and research methodology. Research methods, as it has been stated earlier refer to ***all those methods that are used for conduction of research.*** Thus, research methods are concerned with the methods the researcher use in performing research operations. Keeping research at center of solving a given problem, research methods can be put into the following three groups: those methods which are concerned with concerned with ***collection of data;*** those statistical techniques which are used for *establishing relationships between the data and unknowns; t*hose methods which are used to *evaluate the accuracy of the results obtained.* When we talk of research methodology we not only talk of the research methods but also consider the logic behind the methods we use in the conceit of our research study and explain why we are using a particular method or technique.

Furthermore, the following questions are usually answered by carefully designed research methodology: Why a research study has been undertaken? How was the research problem defined? In what way and how was the hypothesis formulated? What data have been collected and what particular method has been adopted? Why particular technique of analyzing data has been used? and a host of similar other questions.

Significance of Knowing Research Methodology

Knowing how research is done or the methodology of research has thefollowing significance:

- For one who is preparing himself for a career of carrying out research, the importance of knowing research methodology and research techniques is obvious since the same constitute the tool of his trade. The knowledge if methodology provides good training the tool of his trade. The knowledge of methodology provides good training especially to the new researcher and enables him to do better research. In helps him to develop discipline thinking or a "bent of mind" to observe the field objectively.
- Knowledge of how to do research will inculcate the ability to evaluate and use research results with reasonable confidence. In other words, we can state that the knowledge of research methodology is helpful in various fields such as government or business administration, community development and social work.
- When one knows how research is done, then one may have the satisfaction of acquiring a new intellectual tool which can become a way of looking at the sold and of judging every day experience, accordingly, it enables us to make intelligent decision concerning problems facing us in practical life at different points of time thus, the knowledge of research methodology provides tools to look at things in life objectively.
- In this scientific age, all of us in many ways consumers of research results and we can use them intelligently provided we are able to judge the adequacy of the methods by which they have been obtained. The knowledge of methodology helps the consumer of research results to evaluate them and enables him/her to take rational decisions.

1.7. The Research Process

The process of conducting a research involves a series of interrelated steps. Thestages are as follows:

- Formulating the research problem:
- Extensive literature survey (or review):
- Formulating a working hypothesis:
- Preparing the research design;
- Determining the sample design:
- Gathering the data:
- Analysis of data;
- Hypothesis-testing;
- Generalization and interpretation;
- Preparation of the report or the thesis;

Each of these stages is dependent upon others. In other words, the stages of the research overlap continuously rather than following a strictly prescribed sequence. At times, the first step determines the nature of the last step to be undertaken.

1.8. Criteria of a Good Research

Any scientific research is expected to satisfy the following criteria.

The purpose of the research should be clearly defined and common concepts be used.

The research procedure used should be described in sufficient detail to permit another researcher to repeat the research for father advancement, keeping the continuity of what has already been attained.

The procedural design of the research should be carefully planned to yield resultthat are as objective as possible.

The researcher should report with complete frankness. Flaws in proceduraldesign and estimate their effects upon the findings.

The analysis of date should be sufficiently adequate to reveal its significance and the method of analysis used should be an appropriate. The validity and reliability of data should be checked carefully.

Conclusions should be confined to those justified by the data of the research and limited to those for which the data provide an adequate basis.

Greater confidence in research is warranted if the researcher is experienced, has a good reputation in research and is a person of integrity.

Summarizing the above stated criteria of a scientific research leads to derivation of the qualities of good research as follows.

Good research is systematic. It means that research is structured with specified steps to be under taken in a specified sequence in accordance with the well- defined set of rules. Systematic characteristic of the research does not rule out creative thinking but it certainly does reject the use of guessing and intuition in arriving at conclusions. **Good Research is logical**. This implies that research is guided by the rules of logical reasoning and the logical process of induction and deduction are of great value in carrying out research. Induction is the process of reasoning from a part to the whole whereas deduction is the process of reasoning from some premise to a conclusion which follows from that very premise. **Good Research is Empirical.** It implies that research is related basically to one more aspects of a real situations and deals with concrete data that provides a basis for external validity to research results. **Good research is replicable.** This characteristic allows research results to be verified by replicating he study and thereby building a sound for decisions.

Unit 2

The Research Problem and Preparation of theResearch Proposal

2 .1. Selecting the Research Topic

The range of potential topics for social research is a broad as social behavior. The general topic or research problem of a given study may be suggested by *either some practical concern or by some intellectual interest or by both as is often the cause.* Among the important factors influencing the researcher's choice of a research problem, the following may be pointed out here: His/her personal inclination and value judgments, and certain social conditions may exert pressure to select one topic over another (e.g. prestige, recognition, material reward, availability of funds, etc.).

Besides limiting the researcher's freedom in selecting the research topic, the above factors are likely to introduce bias into the study. In developing countries such as India we are more concerned with *applied rather than with basicresearch*, we will here attempt to identify some of the most important criteria that researchers need to consider carefully in selecting their research topics. The following seven criteria could be considered: Relevance the topic should be, as much as possible, relevant to the particular community or society. In other words, it should address a priority problem. In ascertaining the relevance of a topic, the following questions could be asked: How big is the problem? Who is affected by it? How severe is the problem?

Avoidance of Duplication: Developing countries cannot afford to expend valuable resources or similar studies on the same topic. It is important for us to find out, before deciding to carry out a study, whether the proposed topic has been researched already. If it has, there may still be some room for studiesaimed at filling gaps in existing knowledge about the problem.

Feasibility: Having chosen the topic, one also needs to consider the availability of resources (Local, regional, national, and external) such as time, manpower, equipment, money, etc) that will be needed to carry out the study.

Acceptability: the proposed study has the greatest chance of succeeding if it is acceptable to and support the first is political acceptability, while the second refers to cultural acceptability.

Applicability: in applied research, the concern is obviously with whether or notthe findings of the study would be applied to resolution /amelioration of practical problems. Thought should be given to the chances of implementing findings.

Cost-effectiveness: are the resources that are to be expended on the studyworthwhile given the results that we expect?

Timeliness: will the findings be available in time for us (or policy-makers) to make the necessary decisions for action?

2.2. The Meaning of a Research Problem

The focal point of every research activity is a research problem. Research starts with a *felt difficulty*. It takes place when there is a problematic situation and a need to solve the problem. Thus, a researcher must find the problem and formulate it so that is becomes susceptible to research. But what is a research problem? According to kotari (1990:30), *a research problem refers to some difficulty which a researcher experiences in the context of either a theoretical orpractical situation and wants to obtain a solution it.* Often we say that aresearch problem does exist if the following conditions are met with.

Conditions for a Research Problem

- There should be an individual or a group which has some difficulty or aproblem.
- There must be some objective(s) to be attained at. If one wants nothing,one cannot have a problem.

- There must be an alternative means (or the course of action) for obtaining the objectives(s) one wishes to attain, this means that there must be at least two means available to a researcher for if he has no choice of means, he cannot have a problem.
- There must remain some doubt in the mind of researcher with regard to the selection of alternatives; this means that research must answer the question concerning the relative efficiency of the possible alternatives.
- There must be some environment (s) to which the directly pertains.
- These are usually called as the basic components of a research problem. These components of a research problem entail that the research problem requires a researcher to find out the best solution for the given problem, i.e, to find out by which course of action the objective can be attained optimally in the context of a given environment.

2.3. Selecting the Problem

In the research process, the first and for most step is the choice of a notable problem for investigation. The identification of a research problem is an important phase of the entire research process. Therefore, a considerable care must be taken while selecting g a research problem. It requires a great deal of time, energy and logical thinking on the part of the researcher. Practically speaking, several factors deter the selection of suitable problems by the researchers, especially for the beginners. These include limited knowledge of the research process, unfamiliarity with the areas in which the research isneeded, or lack of readiness for problem selection, to mention only some.

Sources of Selection of Research Problem

There are some important sources, which are helpful to a researcher for selecting a problem. These include the following.

Professional Experience: one of the most fruitful sources of problems for beginning are his/her own experiences as a professional in a given field. The day-to- day observation of the incidences in the working place and out of the working environment, which include the experiences of his/her colleagues, their attitudes, home environment, socio-economic status, and motivational level provide rich sources of the problem.

Contact and Discussion with People: Contact and discussions with research – oriented people in conferences, seminars or public lectures serve as important sources of problem. Moreover, active membership in organizations which are concerned with the improvement of a given field usually brings into closecontact with crucial problems and issues concerning the field.

Inference from theory: A research problem can derived from a critical look into various sociological theories. In other words, application of some general principles involved in various theories to specific situation makes an important starting point for research. For example learning theories, personality theories, of intelligence, theories of motivation sociological theories and many others make an excellent starting point for research in classroom situations, in light of this, an empirical research will help to determine whether a particular theorycan be translated in to actual practice in the classroom situation.

Professional Literature: Consultation of research reports, bibliographies of books and articles, periodicals, research abstracts, yearbooks, dictionaries and research guides constitutes invaluable sources of a research problem in a given field. The study of professional literature will not only expose a research to pressing research problems but will suggest the way in which research is conducted.

Technological on Social Changes: Technological and social changes, directly or indirectly, exert an influence in the function of an organization. All such changes bring about new problems for research. For instance, changes my affectpolicy issues in which case they may arouse interest in investigating new policies among the policy analysts or other concerned personalities. In general, the researcher has to make every effort to come up with suitable research problem.

Familiarity with the Subject and Researchers Training: The subject selectedfor research should be familiar and feasible so that the related research material or sources of research are within one's reach. The importance of subject, and the training of researcher, the costs involved, the time factor are few other criteria that must also be considered in selecting a problem. In other words, before the final selection of problem is done a researcher must ask himself or herself the following questions. Whether he/she is well equipped in terms of his/her background to carry out the research? Whether the study falls within the budget he/she can afford? Whether the necessary cooperation can be obtained from those who must participate in research as subjects? If the answers to all these questions are in the affirmative, one may become sure so far as thepracticability of the study is concerned.

Preliminary Study: The selection of a problem must be preceded by a preliminary study. Particularly study. Particularly when the field of inquiry is relatively new and does not have available a set of well-developed techniques, abrief feasibility study not have available be undertaken.

To sum up, the research problem undertaken for study must be carefully selected. The problem selected must involve the researcher and must have an uppermost place in his/her mind so that he/she may undertake all pains needed for the study.

2.4. Definition of Statement of the Problem.

Following selection of the problem, there is a need for defining the research problem clearly. In this regard, there is a proverbial statement that captures everybody's attention that a problem clearly stated is a problem to be investigated in unambiguous fashion. But when do we say that the problem is unambiguously stated? To define a problem means to write it in a clear and precise manner so as to separate it from other relate topics. You put a fence round it, to separate it by careful distinctions from like questions found in related situations of need. In other words, defining a problem involves the task of laying down boundaries within which a researcher shall study the problem with a predetermined objective in view. A proper definition of the research problem will enable the researcher to be on the right track whereas an ill- defined problem may create hurdles.

Prerequisites for Defining a Problem

The following rules serve as the prerequisites for the definition of a problem.

- Be sure that the topic chosen is neither too narrow nor too broad in scope.
- To make the problem clearer and more understandable, static it as question, this requires a definite answer.
- Carefully state the limits of the problem, eliminating all aspects which will not be considered in the study.
- Define any special terms or concepts that must be used in the statement of the problem.
- Definition of the problem involves the theatrical basis and underlying assumptions, and the research question s.
- A good statement of a problem must clarify what is to be determined or solved it must restrict the scope of the study to specific and workable research questions. The most important step in this direction is to specifythe variables involved in the questions and define them in operational tams.
- A good example of a research problem typically could be: "An analysis of the performance of high school Geography students in Addis Ababa".

2.5. Evaluation of the problem

Before the final decision is passed on the investigation of the problem, the feasibility of the problem has to be tested in terms of personal suitability of the researcher and social value of the problem. The research problem should beevaluated in terms of the following criteria.

1. **Is the Problem Researchable?** Some problem cannot be effectively solved through the process of research. Particularly, research cannot provide answer to philosophical and ethical questions that do not show the relationship existing between two or more variable vividly. Therefore, the problem must be stated in workable research questions that can be answered empirically.

2. **Is the Problem New?** As far as possible, the research problem needs to be new. One should not target his/her investigation on the problem that had already been thoroughly investigated by other researchers. To be safe from such duplication, the researcher has to go through the records of previous studies in a given field to select a topic. However, there are sometimes where a problem which has been investigated in the past could be revisited. A researcher may repeat a study when he/she wants to verify its conclusions or to extend the validity of its findings in a situation entirely different from the previous one.

3. **Is the Problem Significant?** The questions of significance of the problem usually relates to what a researcher hopes to accomplish in a particular study. Is it so important? What new knowledge does he hope to add to the sum total of what is known? And what value is this knowledge likely to have? When all these questions are answered clearlyby the researcher, the problem should be considered for investigation. The researcher should show that the study is likely to fill in the gaps in the existing knowledge, to help resolve some of the inconsistencies in previous research, or to help in the reinterpretation of the known facts.

4. **Is the Problem Feasible for The Particular Researcher?** In addition to the above-stipulate points, the feasibility of the research problem

should also be examined from the point of view of the researcher'spersonal aspects as stated hereunder.

a. **Researcher Competence:** The problem should be in an area in which the researcher is qualified and competent. Before indulging into investigation of the problem, the researcher has to make sure that he/she is well acquainted with the existing theories. Concepts and laws relate to the problem. He/she must also possess the necessary skills and competencies that may be needed to develop, administer, and interpret. The necessary data-gathering tools. What is more, he/she needs to consider whether he has the necessary knowledge of research design and statistical procedure that may be required to carry out the research through its completion.

b. **Interest and Enthusiasm:** The researcher has to make sure that the problem really interests him/her. He/she must also be truly enthusiastic about the problem. If the problem is chosen properly by observing these point, the research will not be a boring drudgery, rather it will be love's labour.

c. **Financial Considerations**: Research is an expensive endeavor which requires a great deal of money to invest. In this regard, the researcher should ascertain whether he/she has the necessary financial resources to curry on the investigation of the selected problem. An estimate of the expenditure involved in data-gathering equipment, printing test materials, travel, and clerical assistance needs to be specified. Furthermore, the possible sources of fund must be consulted ahead if time.

d. **Time requirements**: Research should be undertaken within a givenscope of time, which was allocated with careful analysis of the prevailing situations. Each and every activity of a research process requires time, particularly; it is worthwhile to plan for the time that will be needed for the development and administration of tolls, processing and analysis of data, and writing of the research report. While allocating time for a research project, care should be taken for the researcher's other engagements or commitments, the respondents' accessibility, the expiry data of the required dare, etc.

e. **Administrative Considerations**: The researcher has to pay to all administrative matters that are necessary to bring his/her study to its full completion. In this regard, the researcher should consider the kinds of data, equipment, specialized personnel, and administrative facilities that are needed to complete the study successfully. The researcher mustassure whether the pertinent data are available and accessible to him/her.

2.6. The Hypotheses

Once the selection and definition of the problem have been accomplished, the derivation of working hypotheses is the most important step in the research process.

2.6.1. What is Hypothesis?

According to Bailey/1982:41), the term hypothesis is defined as "a proposition that is stated in testable form and predicts a particular relationship between two (or more) variables" similarly, Webster's(1968) defines hypothesis as a tentative assumption made in order to draw out and test its logical or empirical consequences. The above definitions ascertain the fact that a hypothesis is tentative explanation for which the evidence necessary for testing it is at least potentially available. By test we mean either to confirm it to our satisfaction or to prove it wrong. Hypotheses are conjectural statements that ate amenable to empirical investigation e.g. The Statement that 60 Present or, more of theresidents of Addis Ababa attend worship services at least once a week is a statement of purported fact and can therefore be tested. This statement could be taken as a hypothesis. A statement, which is a value judgment, will not be considered as good hypothesis. E.g. Leadership is a more important subject than Accounting.

The foregoing examples entail that research hypotheses need to be value-neutral and be capable of being proven right or wrong on the basis of empirical evidence. Suppose a researcher plans to conduct research on the following topic. Factors that contribute to Lower Achievement of Female Students more than male ones in ESLCE in Tigray Region. To search for the prevailing factors that affect the performance of females more adversely than the performance of males, the researcher may suggest the following hypotheses.

- Female students receive significantly less support to their education than that of their male counterparts.
- Female students sustain significantly higher fashion role stereotypes in schools than do their male counterparts. It should be noted that these hypotheses are taken as tentative solutions to the problem with theunderstanding that the investigation in due course may lead either to their retention or rejection.

2.6.2. Derivation of Hypotheses.

The inspiration for hypotheses comes from a number of sources which include the following.

Experience: The daily life experiences or the day-to-day observation of the correlation (relationship) between various phenomena leads the researcher to hypothesize a relationship and to conduct a study to see if his/her suspicions are confirmed.

Past Research or Common Beliefs: hypotheses can also be inspired by tracing past research or by commonly held lay beliefs. For example, a number of studies in America have shown that college freshmen are more politically conservative than college seniors, suggesting a correlation between year inschool and political belief. Such hypothesis could be used either to replicate the past studies or to extend the test of a familiar hypothesis to a sample of person with different characteristics (E.g College students in other country)

Through Direct analysis of Data or Deduction from Existing theory.

Hypotheses may also be generated through direct analysis of data in the field or may be deduced from a formal theory, through attentive reading the researcher may be able to get acquainted with relevant theories, principles and facts that may alert him/her to identify valid hypotheses for his/her study.

2.6.3. Importance of Hypothesis

- A well- grounded hypothesis provides the following advantages.
- Represents specific objectives, which determine the nature of the dataneeded to test the propositions.
- Offers basis for selecting the sample the research procedures, and thestatistical analysis needed.
- Keeps the study restricted in scope thereby preventing it from becomingtoo broad?
- Sets a frame work for reporting the conclusion of the study.

2.6.4. Criteria of Usable Hypotheses

Hypotheses can be useful if and only if they are carefully formulated. Traverse(1978) has forwarded seven criteria for good hypotheses. These include.

- Hypotheses should be clearly and precisely stated.
- Hypotheses should be formulated in such a way that they can be tested or verified. They should be testable.
- Hypotheses should state explicitly the expected relationship betweenvariables.
- Hypotheses should be limited in scope. Hypotheses of global significance are not usable as they are not specific and simple for testingand drawing conclusions.

- Hypotheses should be consistent with most known facts. Hypotheses should be grounded in the well-established facts. Theories or laws.
- Hypotheses should be stated in simple terms. The simplicity of the statements makes it easily understandable to others (readers), easilytestable, and a clear and comprehended report at the completion of the study.
- Hypotheses selected should be amenable to testing within a reasonable time.

2.6.5. Forms of Stating Hypothesis: The statement of a research hypothesiscan take any of the following forms.

Positive Form

H1 – the academic achievement of extroverts is significantly higher than that ofintroverts.

Null Form

H1 There is no significant difference between the academic achievement ofextroverts and introverts.

In general, when a researcher makes a positive statement about the outcome of the study, the hypothesis takes the declarative form. When the researcher makes a statement that no significant difference exists, the hypothesis takes the null form. It is important for the researcher to formulate hypotheses before data are gathered. This is necessary for an objective and unbiased study.

2.7. The Research Proposal.

After the selection of a research problem and setting proper direction for investigation, the researcher should write out a proposal, or plan for research.

2.7.1 What is the Research Proposal?

The research proposal is a systematic plan which brings to focus the preliminaryplanning that will be needed to accomplish the purpose of the proposed study. It is just like a blueprint, which the architect prepares before the construction of building starts.

Importance of Research Proposal:

The research proposal has the following importance.

- It serves as a basis for determining the feasibility of the project.
- It provides a systematic plan of procedure for the researcher to follow.
- It gives the research supervisor a basis for guiding the researcher whileconducting the study.
- It reduces the probability of costly mistakes.
- Preparation of a full-fledged proposal is not a one-time endeavor. But it is the result of continuous modification and amendment through discussions with experts in the field.

2.7.2. Components of the Research Proposal

There are certain elements that appear as very essential to good research, which need to be reflected in the preparation of the research proposal. These include the following.

The Title: The title of the research should be worded in such a way that it gives sufficient information about the nature of study.

Statement of the Problem: Statement of the problem elaborates about the problem. It attempts to focus on a clear goal. More specifically, statement of theproblem is targeted towards the following: Stating the background facts, which justify the study to be in order, and developing key research questions which may show the direction of the whole exercise.

Review of Related Literature: The theoretical and empirical frame work from which the problem arises must be briefly described. A brief summary of relate studies found in journals, magazines, abstracts and reports should be made. This provides evidence that the researcher is familiar with what is already known. It also helps to avoid the risk of duplication of what has been done.

Significance of the Study: While preparing the research proposal, the researcher has to incorporate the justification for the need of the research.He/she should justify the importance of the study: as to how the results of his/her study still be useful to the beneficiaries.

The following are some of the points in which the justification stresses.

A wide time gap exists between the earlier study and the present one. The need for new knowledge, techniques or conditions will necessitate for replicating the study.

Lack/shortage of information on the topic. In some instance information in the area may be missing or scant. Therefore, the present study may be useful in shading new light on the problem or in filling the gap in the knowledge pertaining to the given area.

Definition of Terms or Concepts. The technical terms or words and phrases having special meanings need to be defined operationally.

Delimitation (scope) of the Study: Boundary of the study should be made clearwith reference to The scope of the study by specifying the content and geographical study areas to which the will be confined, and.

Limitation of the Study: Although a researcher tries his best to design his research as properly as possible, there are externals (uncontrollable) variables that confront his investigation and affect his conclusion. In his proposal, the researcher has to specify such mitigating factors that hinder the attainment his objectives fully. Such anticipated restrictions are referred as limitations of the study. The possible sources of the limitations of the study include.

- Practical weaknesses in the methodologies the researcher adapted.
- Lack of access to the right data.
- Poor choice/development/ delivery of instruments
- Sampling restriction

- Lack of up-to-date literature in the areas.

Procedures for collecting Data: In this section, the details about sampling procedure and the data collecting tools are described.

Sampling: In the research process, the researcher often comes acrossunmanageable size of population in which case he/she may be compelled to draw representative sample by using different sampling techniques. A research proposal should clearly indicate the population from which the researcher will draw his/her sample, and describe the procedure he/she will sample, and describe the procedure he/she will use to select the sample.

Tools: In order to gather evidence or data for the study, the researcher has developed appropriate and reliable instrument(s). the researcher must be well versed in the use of these tools or instruments. The research proposal should explain the reasons for selecting a particular tool(s) for collecting data.

Methods of Data Analysis: In this section the researcher describes how to organize analyze and interpret data. The details of the statement techniques and the rationale for using such techniques should be described in the research proposal.

Bibliography: This is a section where a list of books, journals and other documents is offered. The researcher should list all reference materials that he has consulted in selecting the problem and which he may use during the conductthe study.

Time Schedule: The researcher should also prepare a realistic time schedule forcompleting the study within the time available. Dividing a study into phases andassigning dates for the completion of each phase help the researcher to use his time systematically.

Budget Schedule: The research proposals which are submitted to governmentalor non-governmental organizations for financial assistance should also include a budget schedule. This is a financial breakdown that helps to estimate the cost ofthe study.

Unit 3

Review of the Related Literature

3.1. Reading_for Research

3.1.1. The need for Reading.

Any research activity requires the researcher(s) to be involved in a significant amount at reading. In this regard, Blaxter Hugut and Tight (1996:93) has suggested twenty reasons for reading for your research.

- Because it will give your ideas.
- Because it will help you important your writing style.
- Because you need to understand what other need to understand whatother researchers have done your area.
- To broaden your perspectives and set your work in context.
- Because direct personal experience can never be enough.
- B/c your Spenser or manager expects you to
- So that you can drop names when came to went up your research
- Because is interesting
- To ligaments your arguments.
- Because it may cause you to change your mind.
- Because writers (including you) need readers.
- So that you can better understand the disciplinary traditions withinwhich you are working
- So that you can become better at reading.
- So that you can impress your readers with your knowledge of literature.
- So that you can effectively criticize what others have done.
- Because it helps you in the process of clarifying and framing yourresearch questions.
- To learn about places, you will never visit.
- It keeps you off the streets.
- To learn more about research methods and their application in practice.
- In order to spot areas, which have not been researched?

Seen from the viewpoint of the above stated reasons, you may read both for the delight of discovery and to contextualize what you are reading. Reading for research could take place in three stages of the research project. These include the following:

At the Beginning of Your Research. The purposes of which are to check what other research has been done, to focus your ideas, and to explore the context for your project.

During your Research, The purposes of which are to keep you interested and up to date with developments, to help you better understand the methods youare using the field you are researching, and to serve as a source of data.

After Your Research. Whose specific purposes are to see what impact your own work has had, and to help you develop ideas for further research projects.

3.1.2. Basic Reading Strategies.

This part of the text provides some basic guidance on four related questions:

- Where to read:
- What to read:
- Whom to read: and
- How to find what you need to read Each of them will be

briefly discussed below.

Where to Read

The obvious place to read may seem to be the libraries of different type (eg, public libraries, university libraries, etc). These are accessible, particularly if you might read. These include bookshops, internet centers, etc. Furthermore, your employer, colleagues, supervisors, friends, fellow students and research subjects may have access to relevant materials which they may be willing to share with you.

What to Read

There are a number of sources or types of materials to be read by you as a researcher. The kinds of things you might read could include Books of all kinds, Journals: local, national and international, home and overseas, Reports: Produced by institutions or organizations of different kinds, including employers, representation associations, political parties, trade unions, etc. Popular media: the daily and weekly press, magazines: Computer-based materials: an increasingly important source, which may include-both textbook and journal materials, Memos, minutes, internal reports: Produced by organizations you are studying; Letters, diaries: and other personal documents produced by individuals of interest.

Whom to read

You may be faced with a great deal of materials, which have been written on the subject you are interested in, this may put you in dilemma of where to start. In order to refrain yourself from such difficulties, you should be able to get plenty of guidance on whom to read, at least to start with, from your supervisor, manager, colleagues or fellow researchers.

How to find what you need to read

If you are a researcher tackling an unfamiliar field of study for the first time, you need to be able to get to grips of it with the relevant literature as quickly as possible. Your aim should be to become familiar with the key texts on your subject area and to supplement this understanding with a broader and more selective reading around the topic. Blaxter and his associates (1996:99) suggest an eight-stage approach to help you find what you need to read:

- Take advice from available sources: your supervisor, manger, fellow researchers or students.
- Locate books or journals that appear relevant in a library by asking a librarian. Browsing around or using a catalogue (see the section which follows on using libraries for further advice). You will find that keyword searches on computer- based catalogues are particularly useful.
- Once you have identified relevant shelf locations, look at other books there, which are relevant to your topic.
- Once you have identified relevant journals, look through recent issues to find the most up-to-date writing on your topic.
- Read outwards from your original sources by following up interesting looking references.
- Identify key texts by noting those that are referred to again and again.

- Make sure that you read the most relevant of these and the latest editions.
- As you develop a feeling for the literature relevant to your field, try and ensure that you have some understanding of, and have done some reading within, its different areas.

3.2. Recording Your Reading.

As a researcher, you have to be meticulous right from the beginning of your research project up to the end and even beyond your project. This will save you time and trouble in the long run. This is particularly important when it comes to recording your reading. Finding information in the first place can be hardenough. Finding it again sometimes after wards can be even harder unless your methods of recording and filing are thorough and systematic. Therefore, you should resolve right from start to note down full details of everything you read. These details should include the author or authors, the title of the paper, reportor book, the date of publication, if it is a book or report, the publisher and place of publication, if it is a chapter in an edited book, the title and editor of the book, and the page numbers of the chapter and if it is a paper in a journal, the title of the journal, volume and issue number and pages.

3.3. Note taking (reviewing the Literature)

Once you have identified relevant sources of information, you have to start note taking. The process of note-taking can be done either in the form of paraphrasing or directly quoting the author's ideas.

3.3.1. Paraphrasing

Paraphrasing may be defined as "restating or rewarding a passage from a text, giving the same meaning in another form" (Hult, 1996, P, 43)". The main objective of paraphrasing is to present an author's ideas in your own words. Often paraphrasing fails due to misunderstanding of the passage by the reader orpartial understanding of the passage and trying to guess at the meaning rather than fully understanding it. Therefore accurate paraphrasing can be achieved through close reading and complete understanding of what is read. To facilitateyour paraphrasing, Hult (1996,P.43) suggests five guidelines as follows.

- Place the information found in the source in a new order.
- Break the complex ideas into smaller units of meaning.
- Use concrete, direct vocabulary in place of technical jargon found in theoriginal source.
- Vary the sentence patterns.
- Use synonyms for the words in the source.

How to paraphrase Appropriately

The following examples, extracted from Hult (1996, PP46-48) are aimed atillustrating acceptable and unacceptable paraphrasing.

Original Passage: During the last two years of my medical course and the period which I spent in the hospitals as house physician, I found time, by meansof serious encroachment on my night's rest. To bring to completion a work on the history of scientific research in to the thought world of st. Paul, to revise andenlarge the question of the Historical Jesus for the second edition, and together with world of to prepare an edition of Bach's preludes and fugues for the organ, giving with each piece directions for its rendering (Albert Schweitzer, out of My life and Thought. New York: Mentor, 1963, P.94).

A Good Paraphrase: Albert Schweitzer observed that by staying up late at night, first as a medical student and then as a "house physician" he was able to finish several major works. Including a historical book on the intellectual world of St. Paul, a revised and expanded second edition of question of the historical Jesus, and a new edition of Bach's organ preludes and fugues complete with interpretative notes, written collaboratively with wodir (Schweitzer, 1963, P94).Note: this paraphrase is very complete and appropriate: it does not use the author's own words, except in one instance, which is acknowledged by quotation marks. The student has included a parenthetical citation that indicates to the reader the paraphrase was taken from page 94 of the work by Schweitzer.

The reader can find complete information on the work by turning to the bibliography at the end of the student's paper.]

Referring to others in the Text: In Harvard system, at every point in the text atwhich reference is made to other writers, the name of the writer and they year ofpublication should be included. It is also advisable to include page number. If the surname of the author is part of the sentence, then the year of the publicationwill appear in brackets.

Example, Bloom (1963, P16) describes this...... if the name of the author is notpart of the sentence, then both the surname and the year of publication with page number are in brackets e.g In a recent study (smith, 1990, P36) it is described as.... if there are three or less authors then their family names should be given, if there are more than three authors the first author's family name should be given, followed by et al, e.g Taylor, Barbara and Jones (1991, P10) it is suggested........In a recent study (barbar and Jons, 1993,P10) it is suggested......The most recent work (Barbara et. Al. 1995,P16) shows that..........

3.3.2. Incorporating Direct Quotes.

At times you may want to use direct quotes in addition to paraphrases and summaries. To incorporate direct quotes smoothly. Observe the following general principles.

- When your quotations are four lines in length or less. Surround them with quotation marks and incorporate them into your text. When your quotations are longer than four lines, set them of off from the rest of the text by indenting from the left and right margins. You do not need to usequotation marks. With such block quotes, follow the block quote withthe punition found in the source.
- Introduce quotes using a verb tense the is consistent with the tense of thequote.

- Use brackets for explanations or interpretations not in the original quote. ("evidence reveals that boys are higher on conduct disorder [behavior directed toward the environment] than girls.")

3.4. Organizing Your Literature Review.

Once you have finished collecting and reviewing the literature, you are then required to organize the information in a way that suites to your interest. To this end, it is useful to plan the review out beforehand in not form so that the right order and flow of argument, proposition and debate is achieved. Experience shows that taking precautions to the following points will lead to effective organization of the related literature.

- Develop an outline or topic headings on which discussions of a review of the related literature follows.
- Categorize the evidences of your review in light of tour outline.
- Whenever necessary, try to ask your supervisor, manger, colleagues or fellow students for advice as to what is expected and as to how you can proceed organizing.
- Present a brief summary of your review at the end of this section.

Reviewing the literature checklist

A literature review is not just a question of displaying knowledge and erudition. Rather, it is evaluate by the extent to which the survey illuminates and carries forward the research focus and concerns. Therefore, when the literature survey has been written checking the following points as recommended by Birly and Moreland (1998,P96) are relevant.

- Has the emphasis been given to the most important and relevant authorsand works?
- Are the sources up to date?
- Is the survey critical of authors and their work where appropriate?
- Does the literature review focus on the research and questions?

Unit Four: Types of Research

4.1. Evaluation research

In a very broad sense, the concept of evaluation research simply connotes use ofresearch methods to evaluate programmes or services and determine how effectively they are achieving their goals. The terms like evaluation research, evaluative research, evaluative research, programme evaluations and evaluation are synonymous, interrelated and hence used interchangeably

All the programmes undertaken are to be evaluated for the results they have achieved or failed to achieve. Evaluation research provides objective assessmentof the performance. It is indispensable as it provides the programme administrator with effective use of resources and of accountability for their use. It is now considered as an integral part of governmental as well as non- governmental organizations and is recognized as an important process to improve the working of organizations. Its chief function is to determine as systematically and objectively as possible the relevant effectiveness and impact of their objectives. As such, evaluation is an indispensable action oriented tool in the organizational process for improving both activities still in progress and future planning programming and decision making. It is also a process, which covers aspects relating to the accessibility, availability, and quality of the services and their utilization, their relevance or appropriateness to local needs and expectations, viability of the consequences or impact of the programme.

4.2. Evaluation Research for Impact, Outcome and Efficiency

Evaluation of programme outcome and efficiency may assess whether the programme has effectively attained its goals, whether it has any unintended harmful effects, effects, whether its success (if any) has been achieved at reasonable cost and how the ratio of its benefits to its costs compares with other programmes having similar objectives (Bhatt, 1984). This approach to evaluation research, refers to the formal goals and mission of programme, whether it has achieved what the planners wanted to achieve.

A development programme is designed to produce significant outputs/results of social change and social transformation. Based on these facts, it is believed that experimental designs are best suited for a precise assessment of the results. In other words the experimental designs should therefore be used wherever the essential conditions for organizing it are available. These are basically measurements at two or more points in time (before, during and after the projects period) in regard to both experimental groups (those who participated in the programme) and control groups (those outside the influence of the programme). In evaluation studies that used experimental designs a few used a substitute approach of experimental design. A very common characteristic ofthe studies is that the scope of most of the conclusions of the evaluations is usually emphasized at the expense of depth (Engstorm, 1970). The reports, one observes, are extensive rather than intensive and by and large, very informative regarding efforts in the area of social development.

4.3. Differences between Evaluation Research and BasicResearch

Evaluation research differs from conventional social research already discussed in preceding topics. In a very broad sense evaluation researches are applied social research. By and large, conventional social research is concerned to add to our knowledge, test hypotheses, construction of theories and sometimes to find some practical application in the future social research, in general, and basic research, in particular, is carried on for its own sake. There may not be a practical purpose-to produce results that are, practical, and useful, evaluation research is a special branch of applied research, designed to evaluate social programmes and projects, such as adult/non-formal education, welfare schemes,innovative intervention methods, health care delivery systems, job training programmes etc. the findings of evaluation research are not meant merely to addto our knowledge or construct theories. They are used to decide whether the programmes should continue as it is or with some modifications or be abandoned, whether budgets should be enhanced or reduced, whether staffshould be hired or fired-all based on whether the programme achieved itsintended goals.

Inevitable conflicts arise between programme directors or agency administratorswhose careers depend upon implementing successful programmes and evaluation researchers whose careers require that they evaluate the programmes objectively. It is recommended that programme directors/ administrators do adopt a positive attitude and accept evaluation findings from evaluators about whether the programmes they are directing/administering achieve the intended goal.

As it carried out to evaluate ongoing programmes, evaluation research is designed with a shorter time span than basic research, The social problems are not solved immediately, but decisions about programmes are made immediatelybecause budget allocations and personnel decisions are frequently based on demonstrable "results" Laurence Lynn (1977) points out that "social problems are seldom solved by a single decisive act or policy declaration; rather, policies to deal with them are fashioned incrementally over time in a series of measures which are partial and not necessarily reversible" (Laurence Lynn, 1977,p.72). However, policymakers often have "short time horizons" and wish to see research results to justify continuing or terminating a program. The need for quick and definite answers makes most evaluation research different from basic research.

Although evaluation research is intended to produce immediate results and havean immediate impact, two circumstances often prevent this from happening. The first arises when results are equivocal or contradictory, so that it is not clear what the policy decision should be. There have been many evaluations of adult education, for instance, and they do not all agree about the programmes success or failure. Community Development Programmes have been evaluated many times in many places, and the results are contradictory. If the planners and policy makers are to use these evaluation results, which results, which results should they use? The second situation that prohibits use of the results of programme evaluation arises when the effects of social welfare programmes are not immediately visible. For instance, education was originally introduced to educated three and four-year-old children so that they would become achieving self-sufficient adults. However, educational planners are not prepared to wait for 15 or 20 years for an evaluation before they decide whether to continue with the early childhood education programmes. Instead, they use immediate outcomes; the children's subsequent academic achievement in primary school- and assume that adult educational achievement will follow from childhoodscholastic performance. There is positive but weak connection between the two.

Activity. 1.
Discuss the difference between Evaluation Research and Basic Research?

____
____
____
____

4.4. Evaluation Research Models

Evaluation research has been undertaken on the following two models:

- Goal attainment model, and
- The system model.

The first model starts with taking into account the goals. This is followed by determination of measures of goals, collection of data and appraisal of the effectof the goals. Finally, the initial goals are modified in the light of the appraisal. The second model, on the other hand is concerned not only with goals and sub- goals but also the coordination of organizations sub-units, the execution and maintenance of necessary resources. Within the area of evaluation research, a wide range of evaluation strategies, each withdistinctive features and each applicable to different research problem are available. However, all the evaluation researches can be grouped on the basis of goals of the study. These are:

- Formative Evaluation Research.
- Summative Evaluation Research.

4.4.1. Formative Evaluation Research

Formative evaluation research focuses on providing information to guide theplanning development and implementation of a specific programme. For initiating a programme, certain basic data are essential. First, it is necessary to have date on the personal and socio-economic characteristics of the target population, Second, it is important to be aware of existing services. Third the programme planners should have knowledge about intervention strategies. Finally it is necessary that it should be measurable. To get answers to this question formative researches are undertaken. Formative evaluation research is usually qualitative research and uses case histories rather than statistics to make a judgment. As such, it uses participatory research techniques like observation.

4.4.2 Summative Evaluation Research

Summative evaluation research involves assessing the impact of a programme. The results of summative evaluation researches are basically used for policy making or decision making, such as whether to continue, expand, or cancel a programme. Summative evaluation research examines the effects of a programme. It uses experimental. Quasi-experimental and survey research designs. Summative evaluation research usually uses statistical analysis of quantitative data. Summative evaluations are used to decide whether programmes should continue or cease, and for this reason administrators may resist and evaluators find it difficult to implement summative evaluation.

Formative evaluation seems more desirable because it is used to help the agency administrators formulate their programme, review them; and improve them, Formative evaluation research provides feedback to the programme director about how the participants react to the programme, how the implementers are carrying out the programme, and whether the actual programme is in line with the intended programme. They analyze the programme as it appears in action and describe how it works. This feedback is received during the initial stages of a programme, when it is still possible to change and improve—hence, the name formative evaluation research. By contrast, summative evaluation researches aremost often carried out during the terminal phase of the programme.

4.4. 3.TYPES OF EVALUATION RESEARCH BYEVALUATORS

Some researchers prefer to classify evaluation researches according to evaluators, i.e. the persons responsible for evaluation of the programme. Based on this classification, evaluation researches can be of three types:

a) **Internal Evaluation**: In internal evaluation the personnel and the executive of the agency and the group participate. It is a continuous process, which is done at various points and in respect of various aspects of the programme/project activities. This is an approach to programme/project administration that involves fairly continuous self-evaluation by principal/Director and participants, according to pre- established criteria related to the purpose and goal. Usually, this type of evaluation is included in theproject plan during the design stage and given funding as part of the project.

b) **External Evaluation**: Persons outside the agency do external evaluation. Funding organizations retain evaluators from outside the agency to evaluate the programme/project activities for the purpose of finding out how the money given is utilized by the agency. External evaluators are chosen basically for two reasons. The first reason arises from the fact that the 'outsiders' are assumed to be more objective or at least neutral. The second is to obtain specialists and experts in certain areas, they add fresh perspectives and thinking; they may possess expert technical knowledge and skills that are absolutely necessary for athorough evaluation; and their presence in an evaluation team helps give evidence of impartiality and thus enhances the credibility of the results.

c) **Joint Evaluation**: This type of evaluation involves external evaluators and one or more representatives of the agency. While joint evaluations are difficult, they can be very useful for training agency personnel and gaining their ownership of results.

4.4.4. TYPES OF EVALUATION RESEARCH BY THETIMING OF

EVALUATION

Another categorization of types of evaluation is based on the timing of the evaluation. These types of evaluations comprise a continuous process of evaluation through different points in the life of a project or programme. Three such evaluations are very common:

- **Appraisal Ex Ante**: This is a critical examination of the identification report (feasibility report), which selects and ranks the various solutions from the standpoints of relevance, technical, financial and institutional feasibility and socio economic profitability.
- **Mid-term Evaluation**: This is an evaluation carried out during implementation. Its aim is to draw conclusions for administering the project/programme.
- **Ex-post Evaluation:** This is an evaluation of a completed programme/project. Its purpose is to study whether the programme/project objectives have been achieved. It also includes the lessons to be drawn for future improvement in a later phase or in a similar programme elsewhere.

4.5. EVALUATION RESEARCH DESIGNS

In general, any of the basic research designs, can be used for the purpose of evaluation research with some modifications. However, evaluation researchoften calls for testing of cause-effect relationship. As such, experimental designs are more appropriate for the purpose of evaluation research. Further, true experimental designs use the process of randomization to control the validity threats that can lead to false causal inferences. Therefore, ideal approach to determine the effects of a programme, is randomized experiments. Though it sounds as the most appropriate research design for evaluation research, there are many practical difficulties in using randomized experimental research designs which compare experimental group with control group, in the areas of human resource management. As a result, such experimental researches are considered inappropriate or impossible to conduct in rural development settings. It was often too time-consuming and expensive to identify beneficiaries with similar problems and randomly assign some to treatment and others to control groups.

Another problem about conventional experimental researches was that of the complicated pre-conditions and assumptions of statistical analysis of data, which essentially require complying with probability theory of sampling, which is certainly a difficult if not absurd proposition for social researchers. Finally, the use of control groups, to whom intervention is withheld, has been a source of ethical concern to social work professionals. Thus, although conventional experimental researches are appropriate for some purposes, the drawbacks associated with the method have led social work researchers to find and alternative approach for evaluating the effects of social work interventions and modify and update intervention techniques. The evaluation research designs consist of organization of measures to demonstrate achievement or non- achievement of intended effects of the programme/project. Designing evaluation studies also give credible objective measurement of development, change and impact. The choice of the evaluation design determines the degree of confidence that can be placed in the results of the evolution. Various evaluation designs need to be examined and considered according to their ability to distinguish the affects of the programme/projects from other possible effects not related to the programme/project. These evaluation designs may be set out as follows:

4.5.1 The After-Only Evaluation Design without a ControlGroup

In this study design, the measurements are limited to the target group and taken only once at some point of time after completion of the programme/project activities. This is by far the weakest evaluation design. It is difficult to know whether any change has occurred or to assess the degree to which the changes,if any, can be attributed to the programme/project implementation. The Major weakness of this design is that the 'before' measurements are not taken. Both the groups are assumed to be similar in respect of the 'before' measures on the dependent variable. Hence, it is quite likely that the change in the dependent variable may really be due to the initial differences between the two groups.

The after-only (with control group)

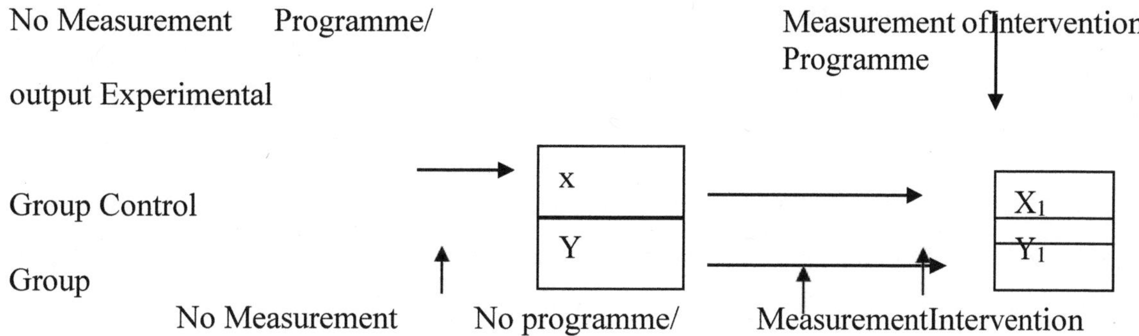

4.5.3 The 'Before' – 'After' Evaluation Design without Control Group

This design involves two measurements on the target/treatment group; onebefore the implementation of the programme/project and another after the completion of the programme/project. The difference between the target group'sposition on the dependent variable (the effect of the programme) is taken as a measure of the effect of the program (dependent variable). But it is obvious that external factors unrelated to the programme treatment have been in operation leading to a change in 'before' target group's position on the dependent variable. The 'before' measurement itself may change the dependent variable. Thus, the major weakness of this evaluation study design is that it does not distinguish the effects of the programme activities and effects of external factors or developmental process.

4.5.4 The 'Before'-'After' Evaluation Design with ControlGroup

This study design may involve one, two or more control groups (groups) similar in characteristics where the programme is not being implemented. The variations in Control group arrangements relate to the attempts to take account of extraneous events, maturational or natural developmental process and the effects of 'before' measurement. In this design of study, both the target group and control group are measured at the beginning and also at the end of the programme/project activities alone.

4.5.5 The Ex-Post-Facto Evaluation Research Design

The ex- post-facto study design is an attempt to detect causal relationship, with data gathered by survey. Here, the evaluator controls the crucial variables only by selecting one, which has already been recorded. For example, an agency has conducted an opinion survey of adult beneficiaries aged 25 or more, taking theirage, gender, place of birth (the independent variable) on respondent's opinion on the effectiveness of the programme of non-formal education (dependent variable). Through manipulation of data the evaluator achieves some control over the other dependent variable (Opinion) and the independent variable (birthplace). In the ex-post-facto design the evaluator does not have very good control of causal variable, study condition, outside variables and measurement of dependent variable. The major drawback of this study design is that the data gathered by a survey is only a cross section taken at one point of time, but the casual relationship in question it the link between the person's birth place and his opinion. This is a casual chain that may be of over 25years' duration and theenvironment in which the person lived during these years may have varied widely from subject to subject.

4.6. USE OF EVALUATION RESEARCH

The important uses of evaluation research are as follow:

- To determine the effectiveness of the programme.
- To answer whether the programme is relevant in the light of theobjectives.

- To assess whether the intervention is effective.
- To assess the effect of alternative/innovative interventions.
- To enhance the quality of activities/programme.
- To determine whether a programme has consequences that is eitherdesirable or undesirable.
- To justify and define the programme in cost effective terms, for fundingorganizations.

4.7 ACTION RESEARCH

Many authors have pointed out the contradiction between the words and impliedmeanings of 'action' and 'research'. Action is a here and now activity whereas research is a planned, future-oriented activity. Research is preceded by careful planning for application of sophisticated methodology for generating knowledgethat can be generalized. Action is temporal and intended to achieve immediate results without any agenda of generating generalizable knowledge. Whatever the strength of this argument, this contradiction is only, apparent. Action research is a well-developed research technique; it is also widely used in varioussectors including human resource management and leadership.

It is difficult to define action research; indeed, the meaning is implied in the two words. Super-imposing relevant research methods and processes over actionthat is here and now is the main intention of action research as a means of solving problems. In other words, action research is research intended to solve practical problems of an individual or a group or an institution through planned intervention. Here, the emphasis lies on solving problems through adoption of alternative practices. Cohen and minion described action research as, "a small- scale intervention in the functioning of the real world and a close examination of the effects of such intervention". On the basis of analyses of a number of action research cases, it becomes evident that it is:

- Situational—it emerges out of situational needs and a solution is alsodesigned with respect to the situation.

- Collaborative and participatory – although individuals can carry out action research individually, it is increasingly becoming a team work where practitioners collaborate and participate with other colleagues in the organization and with the researchers, and
- Self-evaluative—just as action research is self-initiated since it evolves out of the perception of problems by the practicing individual or group,it becomes self-evaluative where the action research team evaluates the outcome of the exercise.

Action Research Contrasted with Applied Research

The emphasis of action research on problem solving has been questioned as a topic of research itself. Nevertheless, almost all textbooks on research methodology provide separate treatment to action research, which indicates its acceptability and relevance, However, it is important to differentiate it with respect to other research methods and designs, particularly applied research. Obviously, if action research intends to solve problems through adoption of alternative practice and assessing its impact, it is not historical, philosophical or even survey type of research. It comes closer to experimental research, particularly, certain types of pre experimental designs.

The Major departure from applied research is on the very intent of the two typesof research studies. Let us see the differences between applied research and action research against a few issues of research methodology (See the table below).

Table: Comparison of Applied and Action Research on Methodological Components

Research Methods	**Applied Research**	**Action Research**

Goals	Creation of new knowledge through generalization	Locale specific problem solving
Hypothesis	Often formulated on the basis of previous research and theoretical knowledge	Not necessary; can be formulated by informed guess of the practioners
Research Design	Sophisticated	Crude
Treatment	Usually, decided and designed well in advance and not changed during the experiment	Interim review of the effect of treatment leads to modification of the treatment since emphasis is on problem solving
Variables	Carefully chosen and classified under categories like criterion independent and intervening	Not an issue—whatever be the variables they are there in the problem situation
Sample	Randomized or representative	Whatever is available sampling is not an issue
Tests and measurements	Necessary to check validity, reliability and objectivity; also relevance of norms where normative sampling is necessary	Tests, questionnaires, etc designed by practitioners can be adequate; however, instruments with tested properties like validity, reliability ect. Provide better information and feedback
Statistical Analysis of	Sophisticated techniques are used	Crude analysis that provides adequate

Data q	not only to assess the impact of the independent variables on the treatment but also to assess the impact of intervening variables	feedback to the problem solving efforts is adequate.

2. Partners in Action Research

There are at least three possible partners in action research. First, an individual development worker or an NGO or an administrator may undertake action research to solve his/her problems in a work situation. The second important possibility is that, a group of human resource /leadership researchers can undertake action research together where they have a common problem, like lack of awareness or motivation, etc. it is also possible that a group of administrators across institutions can undertake action research where they face a common problem. The third possibility is collaboration among practitioners – individual (s) or groups (s) this collaborative action research brings the strength of the two or more types of solution arrived at. In this case, research may take a more sophisticated form that normally it does in action research.

This partnership issue in action research brings us to another dimension. How large an operation can action research be? Well, it depends upon the partner. Ifit is one individual carrying out a problem solving exercise, obviously, the campus of the action research will be small. When several researchers join on one problem, the research may cover an entire institution. Extending it further, when several administrators across institutions in a district or a state join hands to solve a problem, the research may cover several institutions.

3 Areas of Action Research

Action research can cover almost every area of activity of an institution. Let us see a sample list:

- Evaluation procedures – evaluation of programmes and services, use of various techniques and tolls of assessment, etc.
- Staff development – in service staff development programmes, training, work groups, workshop designing, etc.
- Management and Administration—personnel management, information systems management of academic activities including evaluation, participatory management and team building, motivation etc.
- Behavioral changes – attitudes and values through specific scholastic and non-scholastic interventions of practices.

Thus, almost all areas have the potentiality of using action research for solving problems and for improvement of practices.

4. Stages of Action Research

There are four major stages in the conduct of action research. These stages are clearly demarcated. It can be a linear or spiraling process. Stage one comprises actual diagnosis of the problem. Often, the perceived problem is only symptomatic and not the real one. It becomes necessary to go deep into the problem through the symptoms to diagnose it clearly. Stage two is the planning stage where the treatment is designed and methods of assessing the impact are defined. Stage three is the actual implementation, collection and analysis of datato assess the change in the magnitude of the problem. Stage four is reflection. These four stages are discussed below.

Stage One—Diagnosis

- Identification, evaluation and formulation of problems – diagnosing the problem on the basis of symptoms.
- Preliminary discussions and negotiations among interested parties – especially important if the project is to be under taken by more than one individual and in partnership with professional researchers.
- Review of Literature – though not in all cases, certain types of problem may call for reviewing research literature before articulating the problem.
- Modification and redefinition of initial statement of problems – thediscussion and negotiation of the stage two and review of related literature may warrant redefinition or refining the problem statement for the action research.
- Selection of research procedure – designing the intervention, sampling administration, choice of material, and methods of evaluation.

Stage Two: Planning

Stage Three – Intervention and Impact Assessment

- Implementation of the project – actually, carrying out the treatmentdesignee on the sample as per the specifications arrived at step 5 above. This will also include collection of relevant data. In some cases, action research may also call for base line information.
- Interpretation of data – the data collected needs to be interpreted throughminimal statistical or qualitative analysis so that the impact of the treatment on the alleviation of the problem can be assessed.

Stage Four – Reflection

Beyond the factual database results is the role of reflection with the mainpurpose of interpreting the results – the why's and how's of the findings and reflecting on the onward destination.

Although these stages are clearly demarcated, it is possible to interpret them in a linear sequence as well as in spiraling process. Wherever the purpose of a piece of action research is limited to solving 'a unique problem' that is not typical, it can afford a linear sequencing and research is over here and now. Each action research can lead to another level of excellence and performance in the selected area of development. In such areas, action research needs to be seen as aspiraling process.

Naturalistic Inquiry

The process of scientific inquiry follows a paradigm of deductive – hypothetic- inductive approach. In other words, the process of scientific inquiry starts with statements of hypothesis, which are arrived at through a deductive process. Then starts the process of testing hypotheses or theoretical questions either in physically controlled situations or through statistically controlled techniques. Objectivity is to be ensured through selection of representative samples, use of standardized tests and instruments, and use of different sophisticated statistical designs for treatment of data and generalization of findings. On the contrary, naturalistic inquiry follows an altogether different conceptual framework which takes into account the following factors.

Multiple Realities: First, naturalists assume that there exist multiple realities in social situations which exist in concrete forms. They are perceived by people differently and thus become different mental constructs for different people. In other words, realities are taken to be what people perceive them at a particular point of time. Since social situations keep on changing from time to time, the realities, too, keep on changing. Furthermore, since the realities are context specific, they cannot be tangible in a generalized form.

Meanings and Interpretations: Naturalists emphasis study of meanings given to or interpretations made about objects, events and processes concerning social situations. To them, changes in terms of social and behavioral phenomenacannot be identified with the concept of physical movements but by external observation alone. In understanding of human behavior or a social phenomenon involves understanding of how humans see what they are doing or participating in an activity.

Generation of Knowledge: Naturalistic inquiry insists on generation of knowledge resulting from the interaction between the researcher and the respondents. The respondents answer the questions put by the inquirer in terms of their perception or the meanings they attach to their actions. Moreover, interactions take place between the researcher and his/her respondents to achieve maximum levels of responsiveness and insights concerning the problemunder investigation.

Generalization: As stated above, naturalists do not believe in the process of generalization as propounded by scientists. Naturalists argue that in the process of making generalization, a lot of meaningful information existing in individual units is undermined; hence, generalized knowledge does not represent realknowledge. For them, the process of knowledge does not represent real knowledge generation must take into account the differences or the real evidence existing in specific situations. That is why, they take into account extreme cases while collecting data.

Human Relations: In the case of human relations several intrinsic factors, events and processes keep on influencing each other constantly. Therefore, it is not possible to identify one-to-one cause and effect relationships in this case of naturalistic studies. To naturalist's causality in social sciences cannot be demonstrated in the 'hard' sense as it is done in the case of physical sciences. Rather, only patterns of plausible influences can be inferred from social and behavioral studies.

Value Systems: Naturalists do not believe in value free inquiry. They assume the influence of value systems in the identification of problems, selection of samples, use of tools for data collection, the conditions in which data are gathered, and the possible interaction that take place between the researcher and the respondents. That is why naturalists stress that the researcher's bias cannot be ignored and it must be mentioned in research reports.

Procedural Uniqueness of Naturalistic Method

From the procedural viewpoint, the following need to be highlighted

Holistic approach: Naturalists intend to develop a deeper understanding of a given situation in a holistic fashion. In other words, all possible information concerning all the significant dimensions of the situation under study is gathered with a view to portray the situations in their totality. For example, Roleof panchayatiraj in Rural Development cannot be studied in a partial fashion. It has to be studied in a holistic manner taking into account the composite influence of all the socio-economic and cultural factors.

Insightful inquiry: Naturalists emphasize on insightful inquiry, where humans are treated as the sole means of data collection. Qualitative methods like participant observation, informal interviews and discussions, reading of relevantliterature, and daily observation notes and diary writing are very often used for fieldwork. However, the use of quantitative techniques like test administration and survey are not totally ruled out in the process of data collection under this approach.

No a priori theory: A researcher goes to the field for data collection without having any a priori (pre-specific) theory in mind. Naturalists apprehend that ana priori restricts the inquiry to those elements which may have been significant prior to developing an understanding of the situation. It blocks the process of holistic enquiry. The naturalist investigator develops theoretical propositions only after interacting with the field. However, it is pointed out by naturalists that there is no insistence on developing theories afresh in each and every inquiry. Experience- based theories in relation to specific situations may act as preliminary guidelines for many naturalistic investigations.

No pre-specific design of study: prior to fieldwork, naturalists do not make explicit statements on the hypotheses and the conditions in which data are to be collected, analyzed and interpreted. The researcher develops only a broad outline of the study in advance. As the inquiry progresses, appropriate design emerges in the field; hypotheses, mostly in the question form and developed therein; final decisions are taken about the sample respondents/situations during the field work; experiences gathered through personal insights, intuition, personal images and apprehensions are recast into appropriate procedures for analyses are adopted to study the pattern of relationships on the basis of the specific data collected.

Naturalistic Setting: As stated earlier, naturalists believe in conducting studies in realistic settings. To them, reality cannot be studied in fragmented and controlled situations. They intend to unfold what happens in realistic situations rather than studying what can happen in controlled situations.

Naturalistic Method: Main Steps

Different opinions have been expressed by naturalists about the procedural details of naturalistic studies. On the one hand the radical naturalists believe in non-specification of the processes of conducting a study. They take field work as an almost mystical process which is non-teachable. Accordingly, an investigator can start his/her field work after learning about the relevant substantive theory or theories and reviewing the empirical results of some field studies related with it. On the other hand, most experts recommend field workto be made as deliberative as possible, retaining the naturalistic status of the study as a whole. This is to smoothen the processes of the conduct of the study. As stated by Erickson (1986), "Preconceptions and guiding questions can be developed beforehand. But the researcher should not presume to know at the very outset, where specifically the initial questions might lead next" The steps can be organized in the following sequence.

The motto of the social researcher should be to understand the realities by identifying satisfactory patterns in the actions of individuals participating in social activities. For instance, in a social situation, broader questions can be raised, such as, if relationships between a community organizer and the community are fully interactional, how do people give clear feedback to community organizer, or how do leaders influence community organizer or how do the community organizer and people create an atmosphere where most of the community people appear to utilize the programmes/services? The above questions guide the preliminary field work and generate further questions in a given context in the course of inquiry. Besides identifying the broad framework of questions, we must prepare a general outline of the sample population to be contacted or situations to be observed in particular contexts, and draw a sketch of the types of instruments or techniques to be employed for data collection.

Collection of the initial level data: Once we identify the broad questions for the investigation, we may make deliberate attempts to identify a full range of variations in the social and the organizational arrangements related to the situations/problems under study. We may start the inquiry in a broader context of the situation before proceeding to investigate specific occurrences of events in a social set up like a rural/tribal community. For instance, prior to starting an in depth inquiry of functioning of a social institution, we may gather evidence on external social surroundings where the institution functions. This may require us to do an extensive exercise of data collection. After this, we concentrate on in depth observations or interaction with the situation which is being studied.

Procedures for the collection of data: Data collection can be carried out in different phases through participant observation. You may be introduced as one of the internal members/participants of the social set-up under study. It may be possible that real participants of the system like community leaders, people and head of the community, or head of the social institution can act as observers for conducting the study. We can collect data through all the relevant and available source and means such as:

a. Study of available literature, records and documents, diaries,pictures, photographs.
b. Interactions with the persons concerned with the programme understudy, and

c. Our direct observation of and experience regarding the programmes/situations.

You, as a field worker, would make use of purposive sampling of significant situations or behaviors you want to study, as well as the persons you want to interact with. Flexible approaches and followed in the field to identify:

a. The situations where participation can take place intensely,

b. The persons with whom intensive interaction is required, and

c. The people with whom casual dialogue is needed.

As stated earlier, even though a broad framework of sampling is chalked out prior to data collection, the actual process of sampling takes place during field work.

Devices of data collection: You can use different devices for data collection. Such as taking notes about an observed situation, using electronic appliances like tape recorders and video camera, taking photographs and collecting relevant documents and literature on the problem. Planned informal interviews/ dialogues with different groups of respondents can be conducted and their opinions and perceptions can be recorded ether during the time of the interview or immediately after the interview. Daily diaries pertaining to the experiences ofthe field work also need to be maintained.

You have to maintain separate records regarding (a) what you observe in the situations, (b) perception of respondents about the problems/events, and (c) your own perceptions about the persons and their involvement in the issue or programme under study.

Since there is no hypothesis prior to data collection, data are not manipulated directly to test the hypotheses. However, through scrutiny of daily observation records and evidence gathered, you would identify the emerging themes and patterns, phrases, actions, action sequences, expressed thoughts, feelings, etc. this process helps you identify further the meaningful situations to be studied and also the way in which the complete information can be collected.

As we saw earlier, field work can be conducted in different rounds. At the end of the first round intensive field work, you may analyze the data qualitatively, refine the previous questions, and arrive at new specific questions for further verification. This is the stage where you can generate creation context specific hypotheses for minute observation. Moreover, at this stage, you focus is on a more restrictive range of events within the setting, and you begin to look for possible connections or influences between the setting, and its surrounding environment. Again, you return to the field with pinpointed questions/hypotheses. Since the scope of inquiry is sharpened at this stage, in- depth interaction concerning the pinpointed questions takes place conveniently. It should be noted that in the final stages of fiend work, the focus becomes more and more specific along with the development of the working hypotheses.

V) Data analysis: In naturalistic studies, data are analyzed descriptively. The synoptic views of descriptive data are referred for interpretation. More specifically, the frequency data are presented in two or three way contingency tables indicating the patterns of behavior. Occasionally, we use non-parametric statistical techniques (you will read about it Block 4 Unit 3) like a chi- square test, Man-Whitney two tailed tests or rank- order correlation techniques for the identification of certain patterns of relationships in the context of the specific situation under study.

A sound naturalistic study follows a cyclic process of data collection, generation of hypotheses, examination of data, further generation and/or modification of hypotheses, further data collection and verification till specific research questions are identified and the patterns of refined relationships are arrived at. Moreover, the final level analysis of data can provide a ground for identification of specific suggestions for improvement of the system.

Let us do the following exercise before we proceed to highlight the issues and problems related to naturalistic inquiry.

4.8. Issues Regarding Trustworthiness and Objectivity in Naturalistic Studies

Trustworthiness of findings: There have been attacks on naturalists on the issue of the trustworthiness in their process of inquiry. It is said that qualitative approaches may bring subjectivity into the inquiry, and the biases of the researcher may not produce authentic information for others. Moreover, becauseof subjective interaction, valid knowledge may not be generated. Naturalists have reacted to these objections with force and conviction.

In the recent past, there have been efforts to fix certain standards to check the trustworthiness of naturalistic inquiry. The criteria are outlined as follows:

a. **Credibility** pertains of the level of agreement between researchers' data and the interpretations, and the multiple realities that exist in the minds of respondents.
b. **Transferability** is the quality that makes it possible to derive the accurate meaning of information on interpretation available in specific contexts.
c. **Dependability** is essentially the stability of information sought and interpretation derived in different situations on a specific issue.
d. **Conformability** refers to the possibility of studying the collected objective/ systematic information and reaching similar/same conclusionsby different researchers.

The naturalistic approach is guided by the following principles to enhance the credibility, transferability, dependability and conformability of the studies they lead to:

- Prolonged field work can enable one to overcome a variety of possible biases and wrong perceptions, which may appear in one short trip.Moreover, it can help us to identify the salient characteristics of the problem/programme under study.

- Persistent observation of certain typical meaningful features can increasethe credibility of the study.
- Interaction with colleagues helps us evolve suitable designs, share the researcher's anxieties, apprehensions and feeling concerning field work and share with them the growing insights in the field.
- A variety of data sources using different investigators with different perspectives can project a consolidated picture of the field easily and canenhance the dependability and conformability of the data.
- Study of the varieties of adequate reference materials like documents, pictures, films, videotapes and audio recordings are essential for increasing trustworthiness of data.
- Crosschecking of data and interpretations by some of the respondents can enhance internal validity of the study.
- Increasing purposive sampling to collect different instances across awide range of events can be useful in maximizing the range of information and increasing external validity of information.

Substantive description of events in specific contexts can be useful in establishing the reliability and dependability of information and conclusion.

Although the above checks are followed in naturalistic inquiry, there is no guarantee for the trustworthiness of a study. However, such checks can generatea convincing situation regarding the meaningfulness of the study. Unlike a long history of scientific inquiry which has established clear-cut standards for its trustworthiness, naturalistic inquiry has a very recent origin, and is yet to evolve suitable checks to enhance its trustworthiness and authenticity.

Problems of observation: The strength of naturalistic inquiry lies more in the competence of the field worker than the tools, techniques, and designs of data collection. There are several issues pertaining to the experience and expertise ofthe field worker, such as his/her relationship with the group being studied, the ethics involved in the processes of intensive data collection etc. We shall now touch upon some of these issues briefly as follows:

First, it is necessary that only a researcher with a clear understanding of the problem should take up the task of conducting a naturalistic study. Since the meaningfulness of the conduct of the study depends entirely on human approach, it is very important to see 'who' conducts the study and 'how' he/she proceeds with the study.

There have been some problems in situations in which an outside researcher acts as a participant observer. In such cases, there is an apprehension that a stranger who is accepted as an observer may be deliberately informed and invited to observe just because he/she is a stranger. Strangers may notice events that contrast with their expectations. They may affect the behavior of the group through their expectations. They may affect the behavior of the group through their influence while assessing this group. The personality traits of the observersand the situations to be studied are the major factors in developing a close affinity between the scholar and the field and making him/her comfortable with the situations.

The inside observer, i.e., a person from within the institution studied who now acts as an observer, may face major problems in the process of data collection. The group member who acts as an observer may confuse his/her role as an observer with that of a group member. He/she may get a biased picture about his/her group or the institution because of his/her personal/emotional involvement with the group. Then, there are ethical constraints too; they chiefly pertain to the confidentiality required within the group. For example, he/she may be denied access to certain situations or documents because he/she is oneof the members of the group.

To sum up, the investigator needs a great deal of self-awareness and a thorough understanding of the group processes to make the process of naturalistic inquiry meaningful.

Case Study Method

Case studies of social institutions may include the study of different individual units like the family, a cultural organization, a social institution, a class or a developmental programme. In the case of studies on communities, a village, a tribe, a slum area or a culture, each can be considered a unit of investigation.

Whatever the unit of a case studies, it is treated as a whole in the context of specific situations. The wholeness is determined through an abstraction of ideas.In one case, an individual's specific behavior may be perceived as totality; in another case, a situation consisting of group activities may be treated as a whole developmental programme, a micro-credit system, instructional development in a group setting or in an 'individual setting' allowing the possibility of using a single method or integration of a methods.

Purposes of Case Studies

Usually, case studies are conducted for developing a deeper understanding about intricate relationships existing in the process-aspects of a specific unit/units through qualitative investigations. In this context, the case study method is not very different from the approaches of naturalists. So, many a time, the case study method is treated as a kind of naturalistic inquiry. For example, the functional aspects of any normal or exceptional institution may be the focus of a case study or any other approach used by the naturalists. Case studies are conducted with a clinical purpose. They are treated as diagnostic and prognostic measures for clients' treatment. This approach has a psychotherapeutic background. In social research, case studies are conductedfor resolving different problems and bringing about improvement in institutions facing such problems. There can be case studies of biographical type, which aim at giving an account of an individual or tracing the development of an institution, or a developmental programme through longitudinal and prolonged investigation.

Characteristics of Case Study Method

The procedural aspects of a full-fledged case study display certain specific characteristics, viz., continuity in investigation, completeness, authenticity of data, confidential recording and intellectual synthesis. We shall explain eachone of them briefly as follows:

Continuity in investigation: Continuous and prolonged enquiry about the situations is necessary till the underlying factors are explored and plausible patterns of their interaction/ relationship identified. For example, the problems underlying the communal harmony cannot be explored in one go. A researcher may have to undertake prolonged inquiries.

Completeness: A sound case study involves extensive collection of data concerning internal as well as external environment of the unit under study. Data collection continues till the completeness of data is ensured and a completepicture of the unit emerges.

Authenticity of data: A report of the case study must be based on meaningful reliable and valid information regarding the case. Several qualitative and quantitative techniques such as interviews, observations, record surveys and administration of test questionnaires find their appropriate application in case studies. Use of multi-techniques approach to data collection and cross examination of data through different techniques can take care of the authenticity of data. Moreover, since the researcher interacts with the typical situations personally, most of the ethical issues regarding the nature of data, the sample situations, or sample respondents, the nature of interactions etc.. emerge during the investigation. These issues need to be dealt with care to make thecase study ethically meaningful.

Confidential recording: The necessary data, involving personal and ethical issues like relationships of teachers and pupils with the management, discipline, confidential records, documents about the institution etc., must be handledtactfully and every care must be taken to maintain their secrecy.

Intellectual synthesis: Since a case study involves multimethod inquiry and deals with all significant situations concerning the unit, appropriate synthesis of the data is necessary to depict the uniqueness of the unit and to explore significant relationships. A skilled investigator with theoretical sophistication, insightfulness and writing skills can do justice and prepare a sound case study.

Case Study: Main Steps

Most researchers treat case study method as one of the forms of naturalistic inquiry. Therefore, the case study method follows the same steps as are followed in the case of naturalistic inquiry. However, the following steps are considered to be very significant.

Selection of a case for investigation: The first step in any case study is the identification and selection of a case for investigation. It mostly depends on the basic questions of researcher, such as: am I interested in the study of a normal situation with a view to developing deeper insight in the phenomenon? Or am I assigned the job of evaluating the functioning of an institution? Or am I interested in identifying the underlying factors contributing to the excellent performance of an institution? Once the case is identified, then one needs to determine the status of the case. For this, several pieces of preliminary information are collected about the background of the case through the already available sources. At this stage, the initial exercise in setting the course of research is done; it comprises the following: Demarcation of the relevant aspects of the case to be investigated, Preparation of a broad outline of the study of sample situations, and Preparation of the appropriate tools for collecting the 'benchmark' data about all the pertinent aspects of the case under study.

Answers to the questions would tell us whether we have identified the 'case' or not.

Data collection: Now we move on to the stage of data collection in the process of collecting benchmark data about the case, we may make use of both qualitative as well as quantitative techniques like observations, interviews, check lists, perform, open-ended questionnaires, record surveys, psychological tests, etc, every cases, the first round exploratory work is done through personal interaction with the situation under study.

Analysis of first round data: Through systematic analysis of the first round data, we can identify the more complicated situations or problems, and raise pertinent questions about the influential factors. In the case of clinical investigations, we can state various hypotheses about the solutions to the problems.

Second round investigation: The second round investigation is conducted for only those specific questions or factors which are identified through the analysis of the first round data. Intensive investigations about the specific issues/problems are conducted through prolonged observations, informal and formal interviews, questionnaires, cross-examination of different documentsand records, administration of specific tests etc. at the end of this second round of data collection, analysis and interpretation of data begin. However during the interpretation of the data, if some more evidence is needed we may go for another round of data collection. Actually, in a case study, the process of data collection, its analysis and interpretation go on in cyclical order till satisfactory answers to the questions arising in the course of investigation are found and a clear cut picture of the case emerges through investigation. Most case studies aiming at understanding the dynamics of an educational/ social units stop at thisstage.

Follow-up: Investigations should be made regarding the effectiveness of the alternative measures introduced. Such investigations give us feedback on the strengths and weaknesses of the corrective measures. If we find them to be less effective, we should conduct further studies to arrive at some 'newer' remedial measures and apply them to the case.

Scientific Nature of Case Study Method

There have been criticisms against the case study method for lack of scientific approach. One criticism is that the case study method is useful in the exploration of knowledge related to a single unit, but it does not have scope to test hypotheses or confirm any evidence. However, this limitation of the case study method cannot undermine its meaningfulness in the process of generating knowledge. Even though the case study method is viewed as a kind of naturalistic inquiry, this method accommodates the process of hypothesizing in a manner different from that of the survey and the experiment methods.

Generating hypothesis in the case study method: Hypotheses in the case study method are generally found in the form of questions or statements related to the various aspects of the given aspects of the educational process which are tested or confirmed more qualitatively in the given context of investigation. As stated earlier, while conducting a preliminary study on the unit, we may start with certain broad questions since we have limited experience of the case. Further, in the process of interaction with different educational situations, several statements may be generated for further verifications. For instance, in an investigation of the classroom dynamics of an instructional system taken as a case, we may start with broad questions such as: what is interact ional pattern inthe class; and "how is it related to students' achievement?" While observing the interact ional pattern you may witness a very high degree of cohesivenessamong the group members and this could induce you to think further regarding the factors related to the cohesiveness in this specific case leading to further questions.

Testing hypotheses in the case study method: Testing hypotheses in case studies generally follow the qualitative approach, viz., the researcher's insight into and impressionistic views about the process under investigation. However, the data processed in quantitative terms can be integrated with qualitative treatment for developing a holistic perspective regarding the case.

Generalization of case study findings: Contributions of the case study method to the process of evidence-generalization depends on several considerations, viz., the nature of the case under study, the theoretical framework generated, and the extent of objectivity possible. An investigator approaching a case wouldprimarily have the purpose of understanding that particular case in its entirety and, hence, he/she may not be concerned with extending his/her understanding to other cases. However, such an understanding may take the form of further hypotheses which could be tested through other investigations. There are possibilities of considering the findings of a case which may be significantly similar to another case studied at a later stage. There are situations wherestudies of different cases can be useful in developing a new trend. For example, piaget's intensive studies on selective children have generated respectable generalization, but more generalizations may be possible from the findings of a large number of case studies, provided the researchers concerned come from similar background and have similar experience, ideological commitments and interest in certain issues. Although the contribution of the case study to the generalization of findings seems to be neglected, its potential in contributing to theorization cannot be ignored by any insightful researcher.

The issues concerning the objectivity and trustworthiness of the case study method are similar to those of the naturalistic method already discussed in the preceding section.

Unit 5 Research Design

5.1. Meaning of Research Design.

Following the selection of the problem in very specific and concrete terms, you are required to prepare a research design. According to seltiz et al (1962:50), a “research design” is defined as” the arrangement of conditions for collection and analysis of data in a manner that aims to combine relevance to the research purpose with economy in procedure.” In other words, the research design is the conceptual structural within which research is conducted. It constitutes the blueprint for the collection, measurement and analysis of data (kotharl, 1990:39). Accordingly, the design incorporates a framework of what the researcher is going to do from writing the basic questions and their operational implications to the final analysis of data. More specifically, the design decision deals with answers to the following questions:

- What is the study about?
- Why is the study being done?
- Where will the study be carried out?
- What types of data are required?
- Where can the required data be found?
- What periods of time will the study include?
- What will be the sample design?
- What techniques of data collection will be used?
- How will the data be analyzed?
- In what style will the report be prepared?

When it is seen from the viewpoints of the above stated design decisions, onemay split the overall research design into the following major parts:

The sampling design: Which deals with the method of selecting items to beobserved for the given study;

The Observational design: Which relates the conditions under which theobservations are to be made;

The statistical design: Which concerns with the question of how many items areto be observed, and how the information and data gathered are to be analyzed and.

The Operational Design: Which deals with the techniques by which the procedures specified in the sampling, statistical and observational designs can be carried out.

Need for research Design.

In any research endeavor, the preparation of thoroughly thought research design is needed for the following reasons:

- Because it helps the researcher to organize his ideas in a form where byit will be possible for him to look for flaws and in adequacies;
- Because it facilitates the smooth running of various research operations;
- Because it makes research to be as efficient as possible yielding maximal information with minimal expenditure of effort, time and money;
- Because it serves as a framework for the process of reliable and valid data collection, and data analysis;
- Because it saves the researcher from offering hasty generalizations or misleading conclusions; and
- Because it serves as a basis for others to provide their genuine commentsand comprehensive review of the proposed study.

5.2 Characteristics of a Good Design

The questions of good design is related to the purpose or objective of the research problem and also with the nature of the problem to be studied in lightof these points, a research design is said to be good if it satisfies the following:

- The design which is characterized by adjectives like flexible, appropriate, efficient, economical, etc.

- The design which minimizes bias and maximizes the reliability of thedata collected and analyzed;
- The design which gives the smallest experimental error;
- The design which yields maximal information and provides anopportunity for considering many aspects of a problem;

5.3 Important Concepts Relating to Research Design

The preparation of a research design requires an understanding of various key concepts. These are;

Dependent and Independent variable

A variable is an inculcator or measure or measure of the construct of interest. A variable can be anything that has more than one value (e.g. sex, age, weight, income, religion, ESLCE scores) variables should have operational definitions clearly stated.

If one variable depends open or is consequence of the other variable, it is trend as a dependent variable and the variable that is antecedent to the dependent variable is termed as an independent variable. These terms define, in part, how the variable relates to one another. For instance, researcher could examine the impact of heavy drinking of alcohol on liver. In this analysis, heavy drinking of alcohol would be an independent variable and the effect e.g. liver disease could be considered as dependent variable.

Control One important characteristic of a good research design is to minimize the influence or effect of extraneous variable9\s). the technician term 'control'is used when we design the study in a way that minimizes the effects of extraneous variables. In experimental researches, the term 'control' is used to refer to restraint on experimental conditions.

Experimental and Control Groups. In an experimental hypothesis –testing research when a group is exposed to usual conditions, it is termed as 'control group' but when the group is exposed to some novel or special condition, it is termed an 'experimental group' in the above illustration, the group a can be called a control group and the group B an experimental group. If both group A and B are exposed to special programs, then both groups would be termed 'experimental groups'. It is possible to design studies, which include bothexperimental and control groups.

Treatments. The different conditions under which experimental and control groups are put are usually referred to as 'treatments' in the illustration taken above the two treatment are the usual studies program and the special studies program. Similarly. If we want to determine through an experiment the comparative impact of three varieties of fertilizers on the yield of wheat, in that case the three varieties of fertilizer will be considered as three treatments.

Experiment. The process of examining the truth of a statistical hypothesis, relating to some research problem, is known as an experiment. For example, we can conduct an experiment to examine the usefulness of a certain newly developed drug. Experiments can be of two type's viz. absolute experiment and comparative experiment. If we want to determine the impacts of a fertilizer on the yield of a crop, it is a case of absolute experiment. But if we want to determine the impact of one fertilizer as compared to the impact of some other fertilizer, our experiment will be termed as a comparative experiment. Often we undertake comparative experiments when we talk of designs of experiments.

Experimental Unit(s). The predetermined plots or the block. Where different treatments are used, are known as experimental units. Such experimental units must be selected (defined) very carefully.

5.4 Types of Research Design

Research designs can be broadly categorized into three; research design in case of exploratory research studies; research design in case of descriptive and diagnostic research studies, and research design in case of experimental (hypothesis-testing) research studies. Each of them is described below.

Types of Exploratory Research Studies.

Exploratory research studies are also termed as **formative research studies**. The main purpose of such studies is that of ***formulating a problem for more***

precise investigation or of developing the working hypotheses from an operational paint view. The major emphasis in such studies is on the ***discovery of ideas and insights***.As such the research design appropriate for *such studies must be flexible enough to provide opportunity for considering different aspects of a problem under study.* Exploratory research design uses the following two methods. The survey concerning literature and the experience survey.

The survey of Concerned Literature. In this method, hypotheses formulated by earlier working may be reviewed and their usefulness evaluated as a basis for further research. It this way, the researcher should review and build upon the work already done by others, but in case where hypotheses have not yet been formulated, his task is to review the available material for deriving the relevant hypotheses from it. He should also make an attempt to apply concepts and theories developed in different research contexts to the area in which he is himself working sometimes the works of creative writers also provide a fertile ground for hypothesis- formulation and as such may be looked into by the researcher.

Experience Survey. It means the survey of people who had practical experience with the problem to be studied. The main purpose of this survey is toobtain insight into the relationships between variables and new ideas relating to the research problem. For such a survey people who are competent and can contribute new ideas may be carefully selected as respondents to ensure representation of different types of experience. The researcher must prepare an interview schedule for the systematic questioning of informants who are carefully selected. But the interview must ensure flexibility in the sense that the respondents may be allowed to raise issues and questions which the investigator has not previously considered.

Research Design in case of descriptive and diagnostic research studies.

Descriptive research studies are those studies which are concerned with describing the characteristics of a particular individual. Or of a group, whereas diagnostic research studies determine the frequency with which something occurs or its association with something else.

The studies concerning whether certain variables are associated are examples ofdiagnostic research studies. On the other hand, studies concerned with specific predictions, with narration of facts and characteristics concerning individual, group or situations are all examples of descriptive research studies. Most of the social research tall under this category. As far as the preparation of the research design is concerned the descriptive and diagnostic studies share common requirements and as such we may grop together these two types of research studies.

The difference between research designs in respect of the above two types of research studies can be discerned in the following table.

Table 6.1 Difference Between Exploratory & Descriptive Designs.

Research Design	Type of study	
	Exploratory / formulative	Descriptive/ Diagnostic
Overall design	Flexible design (design must provide opportunity for considering different aspects of the problem)	Rigid design (design must make enough, provision for protection against bias and must maximize reliability)
(i)Sampling design (ii) Observational design	Non-probability sampling design (purposive or judgmient instruments for collection of data.	Probability sampling design (random sampling) Structured or well thought out instruments for collection of data.

(iv) Operational design	No fixed decisions about the operational procedures	Advanced decisions about operational procedures.

Source: C.RKothari, Research methodology, Methods &Techniques,1990,p49.

Research design in case of experimental research studies.

Experimental studies (or hypothesis –testing research studies) are those where the researcher tests the hypotheses of causal relationships between variability. Such studies require procedures that will not only reduce bias and increase reliability, but will permit drawing inferences about causality. In particular, when we talk of research design in such studies, we often mean the design of experiments that ensure absence of bias and increase reliability.

Basic Principles of Experimental Designs

Professor Fisher who is usually called the father of experimental design has enumerated three principles of experimental designs: the principle of Replication; the principle of randomization; and the principle of local control.

The principle of Replication: This principle refers to the repetition of the experiment more than once. Therefore, each treatment is applied in many experimental units instead of one. This, in turn, helps to increase the statistical accuracy of the experiments. The following intends to illustrate the principle of replication in detail. Suppose we are to examine the effect of two varieties of rice. For this purpose, we may divide the field into two parts and grow one variety in one part and the other variety in the other part. We can then compare the yield of the two parts and draw conclusion on that basis, but if we are to apply the principle of replication to this experiment, then we first divide the field into several parts, grow one variety in half of each of these parts and the other variety in the remaining half of each parts. We can then collect the data of yield of the two varieties and draw conclusion by comparing the same. The entire experiment can even be repeated several times for better results. The result so obtained experiment can even be repeated several times for better results. The results so obtained will be more reliable in comparison to the conclusion we draw without applying the principle of replication.

The principle of randomization: Conduction of experiment under this principle provides protection against the effect of extraneous factors by randomization. In other words, this principle indicates that we should design or plan the experiment in such a way that the variations caused by extraneous factors can all be combined under the general heading of "chance" for example if we grow one variety of rice, say, in the first half of the parts of a field and the other variety is grown in the other half it is just possible that the soil fertilitymay be different in the first half in comparison to the other half. This makes our results unrealistic. In such a situation, we may assign the variety of rice to be grown in different parts of the field on the basis of some random sampling technique, that is we may apply randomization principle and protect out study against the effect of the extraneous factors (soil fertility differences in the given case.) as such, through the application of the principle of randomization, we canhave a better estimate of the experimental error.

The principle of Local Control: Under this principle, the extraneous factor,the known source f variability, is made to vary deliberately over as wide a rangeas necessary. This need to be done in such a way that the variability it causescan be measured and hence eliminated from the experimental error. This means that we should plan the experiment in a manner that we can perform a two-way analysis of variance, in which the total variability of the data is divided into three components attributed to treatments (varieties if rice in our case), the extraneous factor (soil fertility in our case), and experimental error. On other words according to the principle of local control, we first divide the field into several homogeneous parts, known as blocks, and then each such block isdivided into parts equal to the number of treatments. Then the treatments are randomly assigned to these parts of a block. Blocks are the levels at which we hold an extraneous factor fixed, so that we can measure its contribution to the total variability of the data by means of a two-way analysis of variance. In short, through the principle of local control we can eliminate the variability due to extraneous factor(s) from the experimental error. The entire experiment can even be repeated several times for better results.

Unit 6: Sampling Design

6.1 CENSUS AND SAMPLE SURVEY

All items in any field of inquiry constitute a 'Universe' or 'Population.' A complete enumeration of all items in the 'population' is known as a census inquiry. It can be presumed that in such an inquiry, when all items are covered, no element of chance is left and highest accuracy is obtained. But in practicethis may not be true. Even the slightest element of bias in such an inquiry will get larger and larger as the number of observation increases. Moreover, there is no way of checking the element of bias or its extent except through a resurveyor use of sample checks. Besides, this type of inquiry involves a great deal of time, money and energy. Therefore, when the field of inquiry is large, this method becomes difficult to adopt because of the resources involved. At times, this method is practically beyond the reach of ordinary researchers. Perhaps, government is the only institution which can get the complete enumeration carried out. Even the government adopts this in very rare cases such as population census conducted once in a decade. Further, many a time it is not possible to examine every item in the population, and sometimes it is possible to obtain sufficiently accurate results by studying only a part of total population. Insuch cases there is no utility of census surveys.

However, it needs to be emphasized that when the universe is a small one, it is no use resorting to a sample survey. When field studies are undertaken in practical life, considerations of time and cost almost invariably lead to a selection of respondents i.e., selection of only a few items. The respondents selected should be as representative of the total population as possible in order to produce a miniature cross-section. The selected respondents constitute what is technically called a 'sample' and the selection process is called 'sampling technique.' The survey so conducted is known as 'sample survey'. Algebraically, let the population size be N and if a part of size n (which is $< N$) of this population is selected according to some rule for studying some characteristic of the population, the group consisting of these n units is known as 'sample'. Researcher must prepare a sample design for his study i.e., he mustplan how a sample should be selected and of what size such a sample would be.

6.2 IMPLICATIONS OF A SAMPLE DESIGN

A sample design is a definite plan for obtaining a sample from a given population. It refers to the technique or the procedure the researcher wouldadopt in selecting items for the sample. Sample design may as well lay down the number of items to be included in the sample i.e., the size of the sample. Sample design is determined before data are collected. There are many sample designs from which a researcher can choose. Some designs are relatively more precise and easier to apply than others. Researcher must select/prepare a sampledesign which should be reliable and appropriate for his research study.

STEPS IN SAMPLE DESIGN

While developing a sampling design, the researcher must pay attention to the following points:

(i) **Type of universe:** The first step in developing any sample design is to clearly define the set of objects, technically called the Universe, to be studied. The universe can be finite or infinite. In finite universe the number of items is certain, but in case of an infinite universe the number of items is infinite, i.e.,we cannot have any idea about the total number of items. The population of a city, the number of workers in a factory and the like are examples of finite universes, whereas the number of stars in the sky, listeners of a specific radio programme, throwing of a dice etc. are examples of infinite universes.

(ii) **Sampling unit:** A decision has to be taken concerning a sampling unit before selecting sample. Sampling unit may be a geographical one such as state,district, village, etc., or a construction unit such as house, flat, etc., or it may bea social unit such as family, club, school, etc., or it may be an individual. The researcher will have to decide one or more of such units that he has to select for his study.

(iii) **Source list:** It is also known as 'sampling frame' from which sample is to be drawn. It contains the names of all items of a universe (in case of finite universe only). If source list is not available, researcher has to prepare it. Such alist should be comprehensive, correct, reliable and appropriate. It is extremely important for the source list to be as representative of the population as possible.

(iv) **Size of sample:** This refers to the number of items to be selected from the universe to constitute a sample. This is a major problem before a researcher. The size of sample should neither be excessively large, nor too small. It should be optimum. An optimum sample is one which fulfills the requirements of efficiency, representativeness, reliability and flexibility. While deciding the size of sample, researcher must determine the desired precision as also an acceptableconfidence level for the estimate. The size of population variance needs to be considered as in case of larger variance usually a bigger sample is needed. The size of population must be kept in view for this also limits the sample size. The parameters of interest in a research study must be kept in view, while deciding the size of the sample. Costs too dictate the size of sample that we can draw. As such, budgetary constraint must invariably be taken into consideration when we decide the sample size.

(v) **Parameters of interest:** In determining the sample design, one must consider the question of the specific population parameters which are of interest. For instance, we may be interested in estimating the proportion of persons with some characteristic in the population, or we may be interested in knowing some average or the other measure concerning the population. There may also be important sub-groups in the population about whom we would like to make estimates. All this has a strong impact upon the sample design we would accept.

(vi) **Budgetary constraint:** Cost considerations, from practical point of view, have a major impact upon decisions relating to not only the size of the sample but also to the type of sample. This fact can even lead to the use of a non- probability sample.

(vii) **Sampling procedure:** Finally, the researcher must decide the type ofsample he will use i.e., he must decide about the technique to be used inselecting the items for the sample. In fact, this technique or procedure stands forthe sample design itself. There are several sample designs (explained in the pages that follow) out of which the researcher must choose one for his study. Obviously, he must select that design which, for a given sample size and for a given cost, has a smaller sampling error.

6.3 CRITERIA OF SELECTING A SAMPLING PROCEDURE

In this context one must remember that two costs are involved in a sampling analysis viz., the cost of collecting the data and the cost of an incorrect inference resulting from the data. Researcher must keep in view the two causes of incorrect inferences viz., systematic bias and sampling error. A *systematic bias* results from errors in the sampling procedures, and it cannot be reduced or eliminated by increasing the sample size. At best the causes responsible forthese errors can be detected and corrected. Usually a systematic bias is the resultof one or more of the following factors:

1. Inappropriate sampling frame: If the sampling frame is inappropriate i.e., abiased representation of the universe, it will result in a systematic bias.

2. Defective measuring device: If the measuring device is constantly in error, it will result in systematic bias. In survey work, systematic bias can result if the questionnaire or the interviewer is biased. Similarly, if the physical measuring device is defective there will be systematic bias in the data collected through such a measuring device.

3. Non-respondents: If we are unable to sample all the individuals initially included in the sample, there may arise a systematic bias. The reason is that in such a situation the likelihood of establishing contact or receiving a response from an individual is often correlated with the measure of what is to be estimated.

4. Indeterminacy principle: Sometimes we find that individuals act differently when kept under observation than what they do when kept in non-observed situations. For instance, if workers are aware that somebody is observing them in course of a work study on the basis of which the average length of time to complete a task will be determined and accordingly the quota will be set for piece work, they generally tend to work slowly in comparison to the speed with which they work if kept unobserved. Thus, the indeterminacy principle may also be a cause of a systematic bias.

5. Natural bias in the reporting of data: Natural bias of respondents in the reporting of data is often the cause of a systematic bias in many inquiries. Thereis usually a downward bias in the income data collected by government taxation department, whereas we find an upward bias in the income data collected by some social organisation. People in general understate their incomes if asked about it for tax purposes, but they overstate the same if asked for social status or their affluence. Generally, in psychological surveys, people tend to give what they think is the 'correct' answer rather than revealing their true feelings.

Sampling errors are the random variations in the sample estimates around the true population parameters. Since they occur randomly and are equally likely to be in either direction, their nature happens to be of compensatory type and the expected value of such errors happens to be equal to zero. Sampling error decreases with the increase in the size of the sample, and it happens to be of a smaller magnitude in case of homogeneous population. *Sampling error* can be measured for a given sample design and size. The measurement of sampling error is usually called the 'precision of the sampling plan'. If we increase the sample size, the precision can be improved. But increasing the size of the sample has its own limitations viz., a large sized sample increases the cost of collecting data and also enhances the systematic bias. Thus the effective way to increase precision is usually to select a better sampling design which has a smaller sampling error for a given sample size at a given cost. In practice, however, people prefer a less precise design because it is easier to adopt the same and also because of the fact that systematic bias can be controlled in a better way in such a design. In brief, *while selecting a sampling procedure, researcher must ensure that the procedure causes a relatively small sampling error and helps to control the systematic bias in a better way.*

6.4 CHARACTERISTICS OF A GOOD SAMPLE DESIGN

From what has been stated above, we can list down the characteristics of a goodsample design as under:

(a) Sample design must result in a truly representative sample.
(b) Sample design must be such which results in a small sampling error.
(c) Sample design must be viable in the context of funds available for theresearch study.
(d) Sample design must be such so that systematic bias can be controlled in abetter way.
(e) Sample should be such that the results of the sample study can be applied,in general, for the universe with a reasonable level of confidence.

6.5 DIFFERENT TYPES OF SAMPLE DESIGNS

There are different types of sample designs based on two factors viz., therepresentation basis and the element selection technique. On the representation basis, the sample may be probability sampling or it may be non-probability sampling. Probability sampling is based on the concept of random selection, whereas non-probability sampling is 'non-random' sampling. On element selection basis, the sample may be either unrestricted or restricted. When each sample element is drawn individually from the population at large, then the sample so drawn is known as 'unrestricted sample', whereas all other forms of sampling are covered under the term 'restricted sampling'. The following chart exhibits the sample designs as explained above. Thus, sample designs are basically of two types viz., non-probability sampling and probability sampling. We take up these two designs separately.

Non-probability sampling: Non-probability sampling is that sampling procedure which does not afford any basis for estimating the probability that each item in the population has of being included in the sample. Non- probability sampling is also known by different names such as deliberate sampling, purposive sampling and judgment sampling. In this type of sampling, items for the sample are selected deliberately by the researcher; his choice concerning the items remains supreme. In other words, under non-probability sampling the organizers of the inquiry purposively choose the particular units ofthe universe for constituting a sample on the basis that the small mass that they so select out of a huge one will be typical or representative of the whole. For instance, if economic conditions of people living in a state are to be studied, a few towns and villages may be purposively selected for intensive study on the principle that they can be representative of the entire state. Thus, the judgmentof the organizers of the study plays an important part in this sampling design.

In such a design, personal element has a great chance of entering into the selection of the sample. The investigator may select a sample which shall yield results favorable to his point of view and if that happens, the entire inquiry may get vitiated. Thus, there is always the danger of bias entering into this type of sampling technique. But in the investigators are impartial, work without biasand have the necessary experience so as to take sound judgment, the results obtained from an analysis of deliberately selected sample may be tolerably reliable. However, in such a sampling, there is no assurance that every element has some specifiable chance of being included. Sampling error in this type of sampling cannot be estimated and the element of bias, great or small, is always there. As such this sampling design in rarely adopted in large inquires ofimportance. However, in small inquiries and researches by individuals, this design may be adopted because of the relative advantage of time and money inherent in this method of sampling. *Quota sampling* is also an example of non-probability sampling. Under quota sampling the interviewers are simply given quotas to be filled from the different strata, with some restrictions on how they are to be filled. In other words, the actual selection of the items for the sample isleft to the interviewer's discretion. This type of sampling is very convenient and is relatively inexpensive. But the samples so selected certainly do not possess the characteristic of random samples. Quota samples are essentially judgement samples and inferences drawn on their basis are not amenable to statistical treatment in a formal way.

Probability Sampling: Probability sampling is also known as 'random sampling' or 'chance sampling'. Under this sampling design, every item of the universe has an equal chance of inclusion inthe sample. It is, so to say, a lottery method in which individual units are picked up from the whole group notdeliberately but by some mechanical process. Here it is blind chance alone that determines whether one item or the other is selected. The results obtained from probability or random sampling can be assured in terms of probability i.e., we can measure the errors of estimation or the significance of results obtained froma random sample, and this fact brings out the superiority of random sampling design over the deliberate sampling design. Random sampling ensures the law of Statistical Regularity which states that if on an average the sample chosen isa random one, the sample will have the same composition and characteristics as the universe. This is the reason why random sampling is considered as the best technique of selecting a representative sample.

Random sampling from a finite population refers to that method of sample selection which gives each possible sample combination an equal probability of being picked up and each item in the entire population to have an equal chance of being included in the sample. This applies to sampling without replacement i.e., once an item is selected for the sample, it cannot appear in the sample again (Sampling with replacement is used less frequently in which procedure the element selected for the sample is returned to the population before the next element is selected. In such a situation the same element could appear twice in the same sample before the second element is chosen). In brief, the implications of random sampling (or simple random sampling) are:

(a) It gives each element in the population an equal probability of getting into the sample; and all choices are independent of one another.

(b) It gives each possible sample combination an equal probability of being chosen.

Keeping this in view we can define a simple random sample (or simply a random sample) from a finite population as a sample which is chosen in such a way that each of the *NCn* possible samples has the same probability, 1/*NCn*, of being selected. To make it more clear we take a certain finite population consisting of six elements (say *a*, *b*, *c*, *d*, *e*, *f*) i.e., $N = 6$. Suppose that we want to take a sample of size $n = 3$ from it. Then there are 6*C*3 = 20 possible distinct samples of the required size, and they consist of the elements *abc*, *abd*, *abe*, *abf*, *acd*, *ace*, *acf*, *ade*, *adf*, *aef*, *bcd*, *bce*, *bcf*, *bde*, *bdf*, *bef*, *cde*, *cdf*, *cef*, and *def*. If we choose one of these samples in such a way that each has the probability 1/20 of being chosen, we will then call this a random sample.

Unit 7: Data collection tools

The task of data collection begins after a research problem has been defined andresearch design/plan chalked out. While deciding about the method of data collection to be used for the study, the researcher should keep in mind two typesof data viz., primary and secondary. The *primary data* are those which are collected afresh and for the first time, and thus happen to be original in character. The *secondary data,* on the other hand, are those which have already been collected by someone else and which have already been passed through the statistical process. The researcher would have to decide which sort of data he would be using (thus collecting) for his study and accordingly he will have to select one or the other method of data collection. The methods of collecting primary and secondary data differ since primary data are to be originally collected, while in case of secondary data the nature of data collection work is merely that of compilation. We describe the different methods of data collection, with the pros and cons of each method.

7.1 What is Data?

An item of factual information derived from measurement or research. A collection of facts from which conclusions may be drawn can be qualitative or quantitative can be primary or secondary data.

7.2 Measurements (nominal, ordinal, interval, ratio)

Measurement is a process of mapping aspects of a domain onto other aspects of a range according to some rule of correspondence. Rule of correspondence: If the object in the domain appears to be male, assign to "0" and if female assign to "1". Similarly, we can record a person's marital status as 1, 2, 3 or 4, depending on whether the person is single, married, widowed or divorced; well record "Yes or No" answers to a question as "0" and "1".

(a) Nominal scale: Nominal scale is simply a system of assigning numbersymbols to events in order to label them, (e.g. male/female, catholic/Muslim)

(b) Ordinal scale: The lowest level of the ordered scale that is commonly used is the ordinal scale. (e.g. ranking)

(c) Interval scale: the intervals are adjusted in terms of some rule that has been established as a basis for making the units equal (e.g. 2-6, 7-11, 12-16, etc…)

(d) Ratio scale: facilitates a kind of comparison which is not possible in case of an interval scale, including Measures of physical dimensions such as weight, height, distance, etc …

7.3. Methods of data collection

The methods of collecting primary and secondary data differ since primary data are to be originally collected, while in case of secondary data the nature of data collection work is merely that of compilation.

Collection of primary data:

We collect primary data during the course of doing experiments in an experimental research but in case we do research of the descriptive type and perform surveys, whether sample surveys or census surveys, then we can obtain primary data either through observation or through direct communication with respondents in one form or another or through personal interviews. There are several methods of collecting primary data, particularly in surveys and descriptive researches. Important ones are: (i) observation method, (ii) interview method, (iii) questionnaires, (iv) through schedules, and (v) focus group discussions.

- **Observation:** Observation is used specially in studies relating to behavioral sciences the information is sought by way of investigator's own direct observation without asking from the respondent independent of respondents' willingness to respond and as such is relatively less demanding of active cooperation on the part of respondents. While using this method, the researcher should keep in mind things like: What should be observed? How the observations should be recorded? Or how the accuracy of observation can be ensured?

- **Structured observation**:- In case the observation is characterized by a careful definition of the units to be observed, the style of recording the observed information, standardized conditions of observation and the selection of pertinent data of observation
- **Unstructured observation**:- is to take place without these characteristics to be thought of in advance. Structured observation is considered appropriate in descriptive studies, whereas in an exploratory study the observational procedure is most likely to be relatively unstructured.

Types of observation-participant and non-participant: If the observer observes by making himself, more or less, a member of the group he is observing so that he can experience what the members of the group experience, the observation is called the participant observation. But when the observer observes as a detached emissary without any attempt on his part to experience through participation, it is termed as non-participant observation.

Merits of the participant type of observation: (i) The researcher is enabled to record the natural behavior of the group. (ii) The researcher can even gather information which could not easily be obtained if he observes in a disinterested fashion. (iii) The researcher can even verify the truth of statements made by informants in the context of a questionnaire or a schedule.

Demerits of this type of observation viz., (i) the observer may lose the objectivity to the extent he participates emotionally; (ii) the problem of observation-control is not solved; (iii) it may narrow-down the researcher's range of experience.

ii. Interview Method: Personal interview method requires the interviewer asking questions generally in a face-to-face contact to the other person orpersons.

Telephone interviews*:* This method of collecting information consists in contacting respondents on telephone itself. It is not a very widely used method, but plays important part in industrial surveys, particularly in developed regions.

Structured interviews:- involve the use of a set of predetermined questions and of highly standardized techniques of recording

Unstructured interviews:- flexibility in approach to questioning and without following a system of pre-determined questions and standardized techniquesof recording information. The interviewer is has much greater freedom to ask.

iii. The use of questionnaires: A questionnaire consists of a number of questions printed or typed in a definite order on a form or set of forms, mailed to respondents who are expected to read and understand the questions and write down the reply in the space meant for the purpose in the questionnaire itself. A researcher should note the following with regard to these three main aspects of aquestionnaire: General form, Question sequence, Question formulation and wording,

i. General form:- Either be structured or unstructured questionnaire. Structure- The form of the question may be either closed (i.e., of the type 'yes' or 'no') or open (i.e., inviting free response) but should be stated in advance and not constructed during questioning. Unstructured:- the interviewer is provided witha general guide on the type of information to be obtained.

ii. Question sequence:- it must be clear and smoothly-moving, the relation of one question to another should be readily apparent to the respondent.

iii. Question formulation and wording

In general, all questions should meet the following standards—(a) should be easily understood; (b) should be simple i.e., should convey only one thought at a time; (c) should be concrete and should conform as much as possible to the respondent's way of thinking.

- **Interview Schedule:** It is very much like the questionnaire, with little difference where schedules (containing a set of questions) are filled inby enumerators, Careful selection of enumerators: Intelligent enumerators with the capacity to do cross examination in order to find out the truth very useful in extensive enquiries and can lead to fairly reliable results. It is, however, very expensive.

- **Focus group discussion (FGD):** may be called discussion groups or group interviews. discussion led by a moderator or facilitator who introduces the topic, asks specific questions, controls digressions and stops break-away conversations.

COLLECTION OF SECONDARY DATA

Secondary data means data that are already available i.e., they refer to the data which have already been collected and analyzed by someone else. Secondary data may either be published data or unpublished data. Usually published data are available in: (a) various publications of the central, state are local governments; (b) various publications of foreign governments or of international bodies and their subsidiary organizations; (c) technical and trade journals; (d) books, magazines and newspapers; (e) reports and publications of various associations connected with business and industry, banks, stock exchanges, etc.; (f) reports prepared by research scholars, universities, economists, etc. in different fields; and (g) public records and statistics, historical documents, and other sources of published information. The sources of unpublished data are many; they may be found in diaries, letters, unpublishedbiographies and autobiographies etc…

Choice and sequence of methods

Many researchers tend to use a combination of both open and closed questions, Some begin with preliminary unstructured interviews and continue with the structured format (questionnaire) Question: what are the benefits of starting with unstructured and then move into a structured format?

Unit 8: Analysis and Processing of Data

The data, after collection, has to be processed and analyzed in accordance with the outline laid down for the purpose at the time of developing the research plan. Technically speaking, processing implies editing, coding, classification and tabulation of collected data so that they are amenable to analysis. However, analysis refers to the computation of certain measures along with searching for patterns of relationship that exist among data-groups.

Thus, "in the process of analysis, ***relationships or differences supporting or conflicting with original or new hypotheses*** should be subjected to ***statistical tests*** of significance to determine with what ***validity data*** can be said to indicate any conclusions".

PROCESSING OPERATIONS

1. Editing: Editing of data is a ***process of examining the collected raw data (especially in surveys) to detect errors and omissions and to correct*** these when possible. As a matter of fact, editing involves a careful scrutiny of the completed questionnaires and/or schedules. Editing is done to assure that the data are ***accurate, consistent with other facts gathered, uniformly entered, as completed*** as possible and have been well arranged to facilitate coding and tabulation.

2. Coding (re-coding): Coding refers to the ***process of assigning numerals or other symbols to answers so that responses can be put into a limited number of categories or classes.*** Such classes should be appropriate to the research problem under consideration. Coding decisions should usually be taken at ***the designing stage of the questionnaire.*** This makes it possible to pre-code the questionnaire choices and which in turn is helpful for computer tabulation asone can straight forward key punch from the original questionnaires.

3. Classification: Most research studies result in a large volume of raw data which must be reduced into homogeneous groups if we are to get meaningful relationships. This fact necessitates classification of data which happens to be the process of arranging data in groups or classes on the basis of common characteristics.

4. Tabulation: When a mass of data has been assembled, it becomes necessary for the researcher to arrange the same in some kind of concise and logical order.This procedure is referred to as tabulation. Thus, tabulation is the process of summarizing raw data and displaying the same in compact form (i.e., in theform of statistical tables) for further analysis.

ELEMENTS/TYPES OF ANALYSIS

As stated earlier, by analysis we mean the computation of certain indices or measures along with searching for patterns of relationship that exist among the data groups. Analysis, particularly in case of survey or experimental data, involves estimating the values of unknown parameters of the population and testing of hypotheses for drawing inferences. Analysis may, therefore, be categorized as descriptive analysis and inferential analysis (Inferential analysisis often known as statistical analysis). "Descriptive analysis is largely the study of distributions of one variable. This study provides us with profiles of companies, work groups, persons and other subjects on any of a multiple of characteristics such as size.

Composition, efficiency, preferences, etc..." this sort of analysis may be in respect of one variable (described as uni-dimensional analysis), or in respect of two variables (described as bi-variate analysis) or in respect of more than two variables (described as multivariate analysis). In this context we work out various measures that show the size and shape of a distribution(s) along with thestudy of measuring relationships between two or more variables. We may as well talk of correlation analysis and causal analysis. Correlation analysis studies the joint variation of two or more variables for determining the amount of correlation between two or more variables. Causal analysis is concerned with the study of how one or more variables affect changes in another variable. It is thus a study of functional relationships existing between two or more variables.

This analysis can be termed as regression analysis. Causal analysis is considered relatively more important in experimental researches, whereas in most social and business researches our interest lies in understanding and controlling relationships between variables then with determining causes per se and as such we consider correlation analysis as relatively more important. In modern times, with the availability of computer facilities, there has been a rapid development of multivariate analysis which may be defined as "all statistical methods which simultaneously analyze more than two variables on a sample of observations".

Inferential analysis is concerned with the various tests of significance for testinghypotheses in order to determine with what validity data can be said to indicate some conclusion or conclusions. It is also concerned with the estimation of population values. It is mainly on the basis of inferential analysis that the task ofinterpretation (i.e., the task of drawing inferences and conclusions) isperformed.

Methods of analysis: One or more methods could be used in the data analysis.

1.Quantitative data (association/ correlation, ANOVA, regression)

a. ***Correlation analysis*** -the joint variation of two or more variables fordetermining the amount of correlation between two or more variables,
b. ***Causal analysis:***-concerned with the study of how one or more variablesaffect changes in another variable
c. ***Multivariate analysis*** -methods which simultaneously analyze morethan two variables on a sample of observations (e.g. multiple regression)
d. ***Time series analysis*** -series of successive observations of the givenphenomenon over a period of time

Qualitative data (narrative, in-depth case analysis): it is very difficult but thinking through the fieldwork could help. Researcher participation in *datacollection makes analysis easier.* Taking orderly ***field notes, separating types ofdata*** and ***putting the search*** for analytic categories. Returning to early ***analytical concepts and 'caring'*** for crucial events recorded during ***data collection.*** Linking ***qualitative and quantitative data***

Unit 9: Interpretation and Report Writing

After collecting and analyzing the data, the researcher has to accomplish the task of drawing inferences followed by report writing. This has to be done very carefully, otherwise misleading conclusions may be drawn and the whole purpose of doing research may get vitiated. It is only through interpretation that the researcher can expose relations and processes that underlie his findings. In case of hypotheses testing studies, if hypotheses are tested and upheld several times, the researcher may arrive at generalizations. But in case the researcher had no hypothesis to start with, he would try to explain his findings on the basis of some theory. This may at times result in new questions, leading to further researches. All this analytical information and consequential inference(s) may well be communicated, preferably through research report, to the consumers of research results who may be either an individual or a group of individuals or some public/private organisation.

Meaning of Interpretation

Interpretation refers to the task of drawing inferences from the collected facts after an analytical and/or experimental study. In fact, it is a search for broader meaning of research findings. The task of interpretation has two major aspects viz., (i) the effort to establish continuity in research through linking the results of a given study with those of another, and (ii) the establishment of some explanatory concepts. "In one sense, interpretation is concerned with relationships within the collected data, partially overlapping analysis. Interpretation also extends beyond the data of the study to include the results of other research, theory and hypotheses."1 Thus, interpretation is the device through which the factors that seem to explain what has been observed by researcher in the course of the study can be better understood and it also provides a theoretical conception which can serve as a guide for further researches.

Why Interpretation?

Interpretation is essential for the simple reason that the usefulness and utility of research findings lie in proper interpretation. It is being considered a basic component of research process because of the following reasons:

- It is through interpretation that the researcher can well understand the abstract principle that works beneath his findings. Through this he can link up his findings with those of other studies, having the same abstract principle, and thereby can predict about the concrete world of events. Fresh inquiries can test these predictions later on. This way the continuity in research can be maintained.
- Interpretation leads to the establishment of explanatory concepts that can serve as a guide for future research studies; it opens new avenues of intellectual adventure and stimulates the quest for more knowledge.
- Researcher can better appreciate only through interpretation why his findings are what they are and can make others to understand the real significance of his research findings.
- The interpretation of the findings of exploratory research study often results into hypotheses for experimental research and as such interpretation is involved in the transition from exploratory to experimental research. Since an exploratory study does not have a hypothesis to start with, the findings of such a study have to be interpreted on a *post-factum* basis in which case the interpretation is technically described as '*post factum*' interpretation.

Technique of Interpretation

The task of interpretation is not an easy job, rather it requires a great skill and dexterity on the part of researcher. Interpretation is an art that one learns through practice and experience. The researcher may, at times, seek the guidance from experts for accomplishing the task of interpretation. The technique of interpretation often involves the following steps:

- Researcher must give reasonable explanations of the relations which he has found and he must interpret the lines of relationship in terms of the underlying processes and must try to find out the thread of uniformity that lies under the surface layer of his diversified research findings. In fact, this is the technique of how generalization should be done and concepts be formulated.
- Extraneous information, if collected during the study, must be considered while interpreting the final results of research study, for it may prove to be a key factor in understanding the problem under consideration.
- It is advisable, before embarking upon final interpretation, to consult someone having insight into the study and who is frank and honest and will not hesitate to point out omissions and errors in logical argumentation. Such a consultation will result in correct interpretation and, thus, will enhance the utility of research results.
- Researcher must accomplish the task of interpretation only after considering all relevant factors affecting the problem to avoid false generalization. He must be in no hurry while interpreting results, for quite often the conclusions, which appear to be all right at the beginning,may not at all be accurate.

Precautions in Interpretation

One should always remember that even if the data are properly collected and analyzed, wrong interpretation would lead to inaccurate conclusions. It is, therefore, absolutely essential that the task of interpretation be accomplished with patience in an impartial manner and also in correct perspective. Researchermust pay attention to the following points for correct interpretation:

At the outset, researcher must invariably satisfy himself that (a) the data are appropriate, trustworthy and adequate for drawing inferences; (b) the data reflect good homogeneity; and that (c) proper analysis has been done through statistical methods.

The researcher must remain cautious about the errors that can possibly arise in the process of interpreting results. Errors can arise due to false generalization and/or due to wrong interpretation of statistical measures, such as the application of findings beyond the range of observations, identification of correlation with causation and the like. Another major pitfall is the tendency to affirm that definite relationships exist on the basis of confirmation of particular hypotheses. In fact, the positive test results accepting the hypothesis must be interpreted as "being in accord" with the hypothesis, rather than as "confirming the validity of the hypothesis". The researcher must remain vigilant about all such things so that false generalization may not take place. He should be well equipped with and must know the correct use of statistical measures for drawinginferences concerning his study.

He must always keep in view that the task of interpretation is very muchintertwined with analysis and cannot be distinctly separated. As such he must take the task of interpretation as a special aspect of analysis and accordingly must take all those precautions that one usually observes while going through the process of analysis viz., precautions concerning the reliability of data, computational checks, validation and comparison of results.

He must never lose sight of the fact that his task is not only to make sensitive observations of relevant occurrences, but also to identify and disengage the factors that are initially hidden to the eye. This will enable him to do his job of interpretation on proper lines. Broad generalization should be avoided as most research is not amenable to it because the coverage may be restricted to a particular time, a particular area and particular conditions. Such restrictions, if any, must invariably be specified and the results must be framed within their limits.

The researcher must remember that "ideally in the course of a research study, there should be constant interaction between initial hypothesis, empirical observation and theoretical conceptions. It is exactly in this area of interaction between theoretical orientation and empirical observation that opportunities for originality and creativity lie."2 He must pay special attention to this aspect while engaged in the task of interpretation.

Significance of Report Writing

Research report is considered a major component of the research study for the research task remains incomplete till the report has been presented and/or written. As a matter of fact, even the most brilliant hypothesis, highly well designed and conducted research study, and the most striking generalizations and findings are of little value unless they are effectively communicated to others. The purpose of research is not well served unless the findings are made known to others. Research results must invariably enter the general store of knowledge. All this explains the significance of writing research report. There are people who do not consider writing of report as an integral part of the research process. But the general opinion is in favor of treating the presentation of research results or the writing of report as part and parcel of the research project. Writing of report is the last step in a research study and requires a set ofskills somewhat different from those called for in respect of the earlier stages of research. This task should be accomplished by the researcher with utmost care; he may seek the assistance and guidance of experts for the purpose.

Different Steps in Writing Report

Research reports are the product of slow, painstaking, accurate inductive work. The usual steps involved in writing report are: (a) logical analysis of the subject-matter; (b) preparation of the final outline; (c) preparation of the rough draft; (d) rewriting and polishing; (c) preparation of the final bibliography; and

(f) writing the final draft. Though all these steps are self-explanatory, yet a briefmention of each one of these will be appropriate for better understanding.

Logical analysis of the subject matter: It is the first step which is primarily concerned with the development of a subject. There are two ways in which to develop a subject (a) logically and (b) chronologically. The logical development is made on the basis of mental connections and associations between the one thing and another by means of analysis. Logical treatment often consists in developing the material from the simple possible to the most complex structures. Chronological development is based on a connection or sequence in time or occurrence. The directions for doing or making something usually follow the chronological order.

Preparation of the final outline: It is the next step in writing the research report "Outlines are the framework upon which long written works are constructed. They are an aid to the logical organization of the material and a reminder of the points to be stressed in the report."

Preparation of the rough draft: This follows the logical analysis of the subjectand the preparation of the final outline. Such a step is of utmost importance for the researcher now sits to write down what he has done in the context of his research study. He will write down the procedure adopted by him in collecting the material for his study along with various limitations faced by him, the technique of analysis adopted by him, the broad findings and generalizations and the various suggestions he wants to offer regarding the problem concerned.

Rewriting and polishing of the rough draft: This step happens to be most difficult part of all formal writing. Usually this step requires more time than the writing of the rough draft. The careful revision makes the difference between a mediocre and a good piece of writing. While rewriting and polishing, one should check the report for weaknesses in logical development or presentation. The researcher should also "see whether or not the material, as it is presented, has unity and cohesion; does the report stand upright and firm and exhibit a definite pattern, like a marble arch? Or does it resemble an old wall of moldering cement and loose brick."4 In addition the researcher should give due attention to the fact that in his rough draft he has been consistent or not. He should check the mechanics of writing—grammar, spelling and usage.

Preparation of the final bibliography: Next in order comes the task of the preparation of the final bibliography. The bibliography, which is generally appended to the research report, is a list of books in some way pertinent to the research which has been done. It should contain all those works which the researcher has consulted. The bibliography should be arranged alphabetically and may be divided into two parts; the first part may contain the names of booksand pamphlets, and the second part may contain the names of magazine and newspaper articles. Generally, this pattern of bibliography is considered convenient and satisfactory from the point of view of reader, though it is not the only way of presenting bibliography. The entries in bibliography should be made adopting the following order:

For books and pamphlets the order may be as under:

1. Name of author, last name first.
2. Title, underlined to indicate italics.
3. Place, publisher, and date of publication.
4. Number of volumes.

Example

Kothari, C.R., *Quantitative Techniques,* New Delhi, Vikas Publishing House Pvt. Ltd., 1978.

For magazines and newspapers the order may be as under:

1. Name of the author, last name first.
2. Title of article, in quotation marks.
3. Name of periodical, underlined to indicate italics.
4. The volume or volume and number.
5. The date of the issue.
6. The pagination.

Example

Robert V. Roosa, "Coping with Short-term International Money Flows", *TheBanker,* London, September, 1971, p. 995. The above examples are just the samples for bibliography entries and may be used, but one should also remember that they are not the only acceptable forms. The only thing important is that, whatever method one selects, it must remain consistent. Writing the final draft: This constitutes the last step. The final draft should be written in a concise and objective style and in simple language, avoiding vague expressions such as "it seems", "there may be", and the like ones. While writing the final draft, the researcher must avoid abstract terminology and technical jargon. Illustrations and examples based on common experiences must be incorporated in the final draft as they happen to be most effective in communicating the research findings to others. A research report should not be dull, but must enthuse people and maintain interest and must show originality. It must be remembered that every report should be an attempt to solve some intellectual problem and must contribute to the solution of a problem and must add to the knowledge of both the researcher and the reader.

LAYOUT OF THE RESEARCH REPORT

Anybody, who is reading the research report, must necessarily be conveyed enough about the study so that he can place it in its general scientific context, judge the adequacy of its methods and thus form an opinion of how seriously the findings are to be taken. For this purpose there is the need of proper layout of the report. The layout of the report means as to what the research report should contain. A comprehensive layout of the research report should comprise (A) preliminary pages; (B) the main text; and (C) the end matter. Letus deal with them separately.

(A) Preliminary Pages

In its preliminary pages the report should carry a *title and date,* followed byacknowledgements in the form of 'Preface' or 'Foreword'. Then there should be a *table of contents* followed by *list of tables and illustrations* so that the decision-maker or anybody interested in reading the report can easily locate the required information in the report.

(B) Main Text

The main text provides the complete outline of the research report along with all details. Title of the research study is repeated at the top of the first page of the main text and then follows the other details on pages numbered consecutively, beginning with the second page. Each main section of the report should begin on a new page. The main text of the report should have the following sections:
(i) Introduction; (ii) Statement of findings and recommendations; (iii) The results; (iv) The implications drawn from the results; and (v) The summary.

(i) **Introduction**: The purpose of introduction is to introduce the research project to the readers. It should contain a clear statement of the objectives of research i.e., enough background should be given to make clear to the reader why the problem was considered worth investigating. A brief summary of other relevant research may also be stated so that the present study can be seen in that context. The hypotheses of study, if any, and the definitions of the majorconcepts employed in the study should be explicitly stated in the introduction ofthe report. The methodology adopted in conducting the study must be fully explained. The scientific reader would like to know in detail about such thing: How was the study carried out? What was its basic design? If the study was an experimental one, then what were the experimental manipulations? If the data were collected by means of questionnaires or interviews, then exactly what questions were asked (The questionnaire or interview schedule is usually given in an appendix)? If measurements were based on observation, then what instructions were given to the observers? Regarding the sample used in the study the reader should be told: Who were the subjects? How many were there? How were they selected? All these questions are crucial for estimating the probable limits of generalizability of the findings. The statistical analysis adopted must also be clearly stated. In addition to all this, the scope of the study should be stated and the boundary lines be demarcated. The various limitations,under which the research project was completed, must also be narrated.

(ii) **Statement of findings and recommendations:** After introduction, the research report must contain a statement of findings and recommendations in non-technical language so that it can be easily understood by all concerned. If the findings happen to be extensive, at this point they should be put in the summarised form.

(iii) **Results**: A detailed presentation of the findings of the study, with supporting data in the form of tables and charts together with a validation of results, is the next step in writing the main text of the report. This generally comprises the main body of the report, extending over several chapters. The result section of the report should contain statistical summaries and reductionsof the data rather than the raw data. All the results should be presented in logical sequence and splitted into readily identifiable sections. All relevant results must find a place in the report. But how one is to decide about what is relevant is the basic question. Quite often guidance comes primarily from the research problem and from the hypotheses, if any, with which the study was concerned. But ultimately the researcher must rely on his own judgment in deciding the outline of his report. "Nevertheless, it is still necessary that he states clearly the problem with which he was concerned, the procedure by which he worked onthe problem, the conclusions at which he arrived, and the bases for his conclusions."

(iv) **Implications of the results**: Toward the end of the main text, the researcher should again put down the results of his research clearly and precisely. He should, state the implications that flow from the results of the study, for the general reader is interested in the implications for understanding the human behavior. Such implications may have three aspects as stated below:

(a) A statement of the inferences drawn from the present study which may be expected to apply in similar circumstances. (b) The conditions of the present study which may limit the extent of legitimate generalizations of the inferences drawn from the study. (c) The relevant questions that still remain unanswered ornew questions raised by the study along with suggestions for the kind of research that would provide answers for them. It is considered a good practice to finish the report with a short conclusion which summarizes and recapitulates the main points of the study. The conclusion drawn from the study should be clearly related to the hypotheses that were stated in the introductory section. At the same time, a forecast of the probable future of the subject and an indication of the kind of research which needs to be done in that particular field is useful and desirable.

(v) **Summary**: It has become customary to conclude the research report with a very brief summary, resting in brief the research problem, the methodology, the major findings and the major conclusions drawn from the research results.

(C) End Matter

At the end of the report, appendices should be enlisted in respect of all technical data such as questionnaires, sample information, mathematical derivations and the like ones. Bibliography of sources consulted should also be given. Index (analphabetical listing of names, places and topics along with the numbers of the pages in a book or report on which they are mentioned or discussed) should invariably be given at the end of the report. The value of index lies in the fact that it works as a guide to the reader for the contents in the report.

Printed by Libri Plureos GmbH in Hamburg,
Germany